[ROSE]

CLYDE PHILLIP WACHSBERGER
AND THEODORE JAMES, JR.
PHOTOGRAPHS BY HARRY HARALAMBOU

HARRY N. ABRAMS, INC., PUBLISHERS

For Charles Randall Dean

EDITOR: Sharon AvRutick
DESIGNER: Helene Silverman
PRODUCTION MANAGER: Justine Keefe

Library of Congress Cataloging-in-Publication Data

Wachsberger, Clyde.
  Rose / by Clyde Phillip Wachsberger and Theodore James, Jr.
photographs by Harry Haralambou.
    p. cm.
Includes bibliographical references (p.   ) and index.
ISBN 0-8109-5007-3 (hardcover)
1. Roses. 2. Rose culture. I. James, Theodore. II. Haralambou, Harry.
III. Title.

SB411.W33 2004
635.9'33734—dc22

2003020357

Printed and bound in China

10 9 8 7 6 5 4 3 2 1

Harry N. Abrams, Inc.
100 Fifth Avenue
New York, N.Y. 10011
www.abramsbooks.com

Abrams is a subsidiary of
LA MARTINIÈRE
GROUPE

PAGE 1: ALWAYS IN DEMAND AND OFTEN SOLD OUT EARLY IN THE SEASON, THE THORNLESS
BOURBON CLIMBER 'ZÉPHIRINE DROUHIN' IS VIVID DEEP PINK AND POWERFULLY SCENTED.
BELOVED SINCE 1868, THIS OLD-FASHIONED ROSE IS HAPPILY INCLUDED ALONGSIDE HARDY
BANANAS IN THIS VERY "TODAY" NORTHERN TROPICAL GARDEN. PAGE 2: *ROSA RUBRIFOLIA*, ALSO
SOLD AS *ROSA GLAUCA*, IS THE SPECIES ROSE MOST WIDELY GROWN IN GARDENS, CHERISHED
FOR ITS FOLIAGE MORE THAN ITS FLOWERS. NEW GROWTH EMERGES A RICH PURPLE THEN FADES
THROUGH PLUM TO A HANDSOME BLUISH-GRAY.

CONTENTS

Anatomy of the Rose

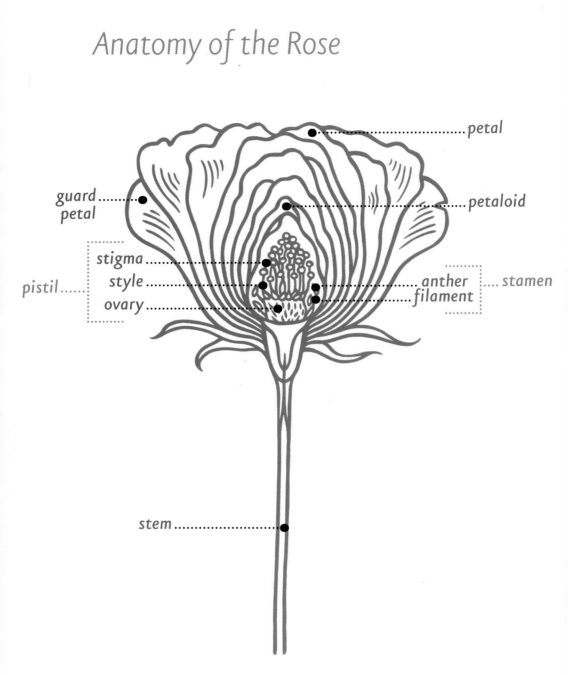

petal

guard
petal

petaloid

pistil

stigma

style

ovary

anther
filament

stamen

stem

ILLUSTRATION: MEGAN CASH

OPPOSITE: HYBRID TEA ROSE 'PRISTINE' HAS EXQUISITELY FORMED BUDS AND FLOWERS TINTED
IN THE SUNLIT COLORS OF A PASSING CLOUD. INTRODUCED IN 1978, THIS VIGOROUS, HEALTHY
SHRUB HAS REMAINED A FAVORITE.

INTRODUCTION

THE ROSE is considered the Queen of the Flowers. Gardeners the world over dedicate the place of honor to their roses and speak of these regal flowers with a loyalty, awe, and blind admiration usually reserved for monarchs. Yet, for others even the thought of growing roses evokes a worrisome image of lifelong servitude devoted to the health, happiness, and well-being of a tyrannical shrub. True, the rose demands a certain amount of respect, but if given a sunny, well-drained site with plenty of room and good air circulation it can be a benign and beautiful ruler, showering fragrant blossoms upon all who come to pay their respects.

Originally native to the Northern Hemisphere, roses are now grown on every continent, outdoors in temperate climates, and indoors or in greenhouses where the weather is not to their liking. A favorite subject of poets and painters since earliest recorded time, they have become cherished both in the garden and as cut flowers. But their familiarity has never lessened the power of their beauty and fragrance to conjure up romance and nostalgia.

A dozen red roses speak a language of their own, whether presented on an anniversary, tossed from the audience to a reigning diva, or delivered without a card to someone who deserves an apology. And yet a single red rose can say just as much!

It is a rose that sets many a fairy tale off on a journey toward an instructive moral, and it is a rose that directs many a romance onto a thorny path. A rose is often the beginning of a song, a poem, a tragedy, a comedy, a memory.

More than anything, a rose is often the beginning of a garden.

The intoxicating perfume of *Rosa rugosa*, naturalized here along a beach in Peconic, New York, is carried far on the sea breeze.

1 Roses in History

ROSES, MEMBERS of the genus *Rosa*, are native to the Northern Hemisphere, with about 150 species originating in Europe, Asia, and North America. These wild Species roses generally have simple flowers with a single row of five petals mostly in pastel shades of pink, yellow, deep rose, or pure white. A few have pom-pom flowers with many petals. Some are intensely fragrant. All the roses we know today, no matter how complex their flowers and no matter how brilliant their colors, were hybridized from these wild Species roses.

The Greek myth of Aphrodite recounts that as the beautiful goddess of love emerged from the foam of a wave, a rose bush sprung from the earth. When Aphrodite stepped ashore, a thorn pierced her foot, and it was a drop of the goddess' blood that stained roses red.

As early as the second millennium BC, artists were depicting roses in the frescoes of the Minoan palace at Knossos, on the island of Crete. In the seventh century BC the Greek poet Sappho declared the rose to be the Queen of the Flowers. Clearly the flower was already cherished, and ancient gardeners being gardeners, they must have wanted to grow ever more beautiful varieties.

The Greek word for roses, *rhodon*, was a popular choice for place names, the most famous being the island of Rhodes, site of the ancient Colossus. Rhodes was known throughout the ancient world for the fragrance of its roses, said to perfume the entire island. Crushed rose petals were a popular local product.

Theophrastus, a Greek naturalist writing in the fourth century BC, described the known varieties of roses. He gave instructions on how to propagate roses from cuttings and by digging up and replanting suckers, and he explained how they could also be grown from seed. He advised that frequent transplanting improved the vigor of rose bushes and he also advocated the alarming practice of burning them to the ground every few years to encourage new growth. Theophrastus willed his garden to his slaves with the stipulation that they continue caring for his plants.

11

FLORIBUNDAS ARE LOVED FOR THEIR REMARKABLE RANGE OF UNUSUAL COLORS, INCLUDING TANS, BROWNS, AND SMOKY MAUVES. THE SUBTLE HUES OF 'HOT COCOA' ARE HARD TO CATCH ON FILM AND EVEN HARDER TO DESCRIBE, BUT THEY ARE EASY TO ADMIRE IN THE GARDEN.

The Greeks began cultivating roses in the mild climate of North Africa and introduced roses to the Egyptians under Alexander the Great. The Ptolemaic rulers Alexander installed in Egypt continued to popularize the flower in their new realm.

Roses became the flower of choice for the neck garlands and crowns that Greek women fashioned for boys and men to wear. Ancient commentators mention the fragrance of these accessories, noting that some men carried small bags of rose petals to smell from time to time.

The ancient Greeks did not understand that plants could be hybridized through cross-pollination, but they did collect different wild cultivars of roses to grow in their gardens so that they might have a variety of flowers and bloom seasons.

"The twice-blooming roses of Paestum," from a Greek colony in southern Italy, were famous for a very particular reason: they bloomed in the spring and again in the fall. Paestum farmers made a good living selling these roses (perhaps *Rosa damascena bifera*, the 'Autumn Damask' still available today), either as cut flowers when no others were in bloom, or as plants for export. This repeat-blooming rose was one of the treasures of the ancient world.

The Romans were as fond of roses as the Greeks, also stressing the importance of fragrance as well as beauty in their roses. The flowers were worn woven into necklaces and headbands. (Some hint that Julius Caesar wore a crown of roses to hide his baldness.) Roses were also made into indoor decorations. A second-century sales receipt from Roman Egypt records a request for four thousand roses for a wedding. A popular and particularly excessive effect was achieved by suspending millions of rose petals in swags of fabric and releasing them onto the guests at the height of a party. Some guests actually suffocated under the petals at an infamous feast thrown by the Emperor Heliogabalus.

Rose petals were also used in perfumes and beauty preparations and for medicinal purposes. The fruits, or hips, as well as the petals were used for flavoring delicacies.

To satisfy the demand, nurseries all over Italy and in the Roman provinces and colonies grew as many varieties as possible to have flowers over an extended season. Like the Greeks, Romans collected roses with varying bloom times from across the empire. Contemporary gardening

treatises listed the earliest and latest blooming types. Romans grew roses in hothouses to extend the season, and encouraged early bloom on garden roses by pouring warm water into a trench around their roots.

While the Romans were growing the available roses in their gardens, almost half a globe away the ancient Chinese were cultivating their own varieties. These China roses had two traits that the Western roses lacked: they bloomed throughout the season in warm climates; and some were yellow. When these repeat-blooming roses were brought to France and England in the early nineteenth century and cross-pollination was scientifically practiced, garden roses were changed forever.

In Islam, too, the rose was revered. In the walled gardens of the Middle East, where fragrance was so important, roses unknown in Europe were cultivated for their beauty and scent. Here, Western travelers encountered not only yellow, but bicolored roses as well. One account describes a rose that had red, yellow, and white blossoms all on the same branch, perhaps a relative of the famous China rose 'Mutabilis.'

With the rise of Christianity in the West, there was a backlash against all things pagan, and the rose, with its inevitable associations

THE LEGENDARY 'PAUL'S HIMALAYAN MUSK' CAN CLIMB INTO THE TALLEST TREES, TURNING THEM INTO CLOUDS OF PINK AGAINST THE SKY. HERE IT IS BEHAVING ITSELF, ADORNING THE ENTRANCE INTO DIANNE BENT'S HERB GARDEN.

with extravagant excess, was at first disparaged. But rather than do without the beautiful flower of Venus, the Christian faithful decided to associate the rose with the Virgin Mary.

In fifteenth-century England, roses were chosen as emblems of warring factions: the white Alba rose represented the House of York, and a deep-pink Gallica represented the House of Lancaster in what is known as the War of the Roses. Today there is a bicolor rose known as 'York and Lancaster.'

Although the French and the English became the most important breeders of roses, the science of hybridizing roses from seed may have started in the Netherlands. Dutch nurserymen worked with the Gallicas and were already offering many cultivars by the middle of the eighteenth century. These roses were introduced into France, where they were then further hybridized.

Toward the end of the eighteenth century several China roses were finally imported to England, Belgium, and Holland, where they created a flurry of competitive hybridization in the gardening world. That the China roses were too tender to survive except in the south of the Mediterranean countries did not deter the hybridizers, who grew them in hothouses and used them to cross-pollinate the hardier garden roses. The resulting hybrids were crossed with each other or with one of the parents. Remarkable new roses began to appear by the hundreds.

Publicity is the most powerful tool in achieving fame, and the rose breeders at the turn of the nineteenth century were blessed with the extraordinary good fortune of having Napoleon's Empress Josephine as their champion. Josephine loved roses, and was determined to grow every known variety in her personal garden at Malmaison, her chateau near Paris. She ordered roses from every corner of her husband's far-reaching empire, and beyond—even from English nurseries during the height of hostilities, spending a fortune one year at Lee & Kennedy of Hammersmith. Her deliveries were protected through heavily blockaded waters by order of the British Admiralty.

In a stroke of genius Josephine commissioned the well-known painter Pierre Joseph Redouté to capture her roses in watercolor

DAVID AUSTIN HYBRIDIZED MODERN ROSES WITH OLD GARDEN ROSES TO ACHIEVE THE CHARM OF OLD-FASHIONED ROSES ON HARDY BUSHES THAT BLOOM ALL SUMMER LONG. THIS IS ENGLISH ROSE 'GEOFF HAMILTON.'

portraits. *Les Roses* was published in 1817, three years after Josephine's death, with gorgeous reproductions of Redouté's watercolors accompanied by extensive botanical text. It was a best seller, a fitting tribute to the woman who had championed roses and encouraged hybridizers to seek all their possible permutations. When Napoleon's empire collapsed, the British had orders not to touch Malmaison, but after her death Josephine's garden eventually fell into neglect. It was not until 1843, when a sumptuously fragrant and beautiful new rose was introduced as 'Souvenir de la Malmaison,' that Josephine became properly memorialized for her extraordinary gift to all lovers of roses who followed.

And follow they did, with a frenzy. Gardeners all over Europe, and especially in England, clamored for more new roses. One gardener in England reportedly ordered a thousand bushes at a guinea a piece. In America an 1822 catalogue from William Prince's nursery in Flushing, New York, had offered 170 different roses at $2 a piece, but by 1846 was boasting 1,600 varieties. By 1900 the French National Rose Museum, the Roseraie de l'Hay, listed more than three thousand varieties.

The first popular crosses created in the quest for a repeat-blooming rose that would be hardy in Europe were known as Hybrid Chinas. While these proved to bloom only once, they were remarkably vigorous and hardy, and their flowers were often gorgeous and deliciously fragrant. Hybrid Chinas, which are only rarely offered today, were further crossed and recrossed with old European Gallica, Alba, Centifolia, and Species roses.

Along with the staggering number of new roses developed in the nineteenth century came a bewildering number of new categories, groups, and classes. The Hybrid Perpetual roses in particular caused a big stir. Not as reliably repeat-blooming as the China roses, these plants nevertheless did offer sporadic continual bloom after the first big flush in early summer. From these roses were developed the modern repeat-blooming Hybrid Teas, the first of which is believed to be 'La France' in 1867.

Introducing the China's yellow hues into hardy European garden roses remained a challenge until the turn of the nineteenth century, when a Hybrid Perpetual called 'Antoine Ducher' was crossed with the yellow Species *R. foetida* and the resulting seedling bloomed in yellows and corals. This line was rebred with the early Hybrid Teas to begin the dynasty of today's Modern Hybrid Teas.

By the early years of the twentieth century a gardener could choose between the famous old roses remembered from childhood and the hundreds of new introductions every year touted with all the fanfare appropriate to movie stars. The preference for novelty became clear. Breeders quickly turned their attention to fashionable trends, and many once-popular roses disappeared from commerce, often because they bloomed only once in the season, but also simply because they were old-fashioned. It didn't seem to matter that the new roses never had the same perfumes as the old roses, or that some might be tender and prone to disease. They were new, and they bloomed all summer. Dig up that rose dedicated to some old French empress and plant 'Amelia Earhart,' brand new in 1932, repeat-blooming, strongly fragrant, and Modern!

Through the twentieth century the trend was toward carefree, disease-free, hardy, vigorous roses that might be grown like any other shrubs as hedges or backgrounds to flower beds. Often scent and delicacy of coloring were sacrificed to easy maintenance and continual bloom.

Still, the old roses lived on in hand-me-down gardens and neglected cemeteries and parks. Beginning in the mid 1950s dedicated rose historians began to save these old beauties, taking cuttings and starting new plants. More gardeners came to understand their charm and were seduced by their extraordinary perfumes, and these once-famous roses regained popularity. In the 1970s David Austin, an English breeder, began recrossing old roses with modern Hybrid Teas and Floribundas and finally achieved roses that had the look and fragrance of the old-fashioned types but the continual bloom of the Modern. The popularity of his "English Roses" soared through the end of the twentieth century —they have now eclipsed the Hybrid Teas—opening the door to more experimentation. Imagine what extraordinary new roses will be available fifty years from now. Perhaps finally the elusive blue rose!

2 Selecting Roses

THE MANY categories of roses and the thousands of cultivars, often with foreign names, are both daunting and confusing. There is a dispute as to which category some roses belong, and others may be known by more than one name. Some catalogues divide roses into "climbing" and "bush" categories, but there might be a variety with the same name in both. Further, some roses will be listed in one catalogue as a member of one group and differently in another.

All this confusion occurs amid an overload of historical information, including dates of introduction and the names of the hybridizers, much of which is important only to rose historians. An understanding of the different groups will facilitate ordering from catalogues, but unless you're creating a historical restoration, you do not need to know a rose's pedigree.

The American Rose Society was founded in 1930 with the intention of untangling the situation by describing in uniform terms all the roses known in world commerce. (Today the ARS provides its members with a monthly magazine and an annual up-to-date compendium, as well as other information. To learn more, contact the society at P.O. Box 30,000, Shreveport, LA 71130, or www.ars.org.)

The ARS created three basic classifications—Species roses, Old Garden roses, and Modern roses—to which we conform in this book, but do keep in mind that not all catalogues do so exactly.

You should choose a rose for your garden based purely on the attributes you find particularly appealing. Be won over by a photograph, and then check the description and growth habit. Choose a plant for its size, color or shape of flower, and appropriateness to your climate. Just as you might with a lifetime companion, look for those characteristics that attract you, and don't concern yourself with parents, family, and certainly not lineage. If the rose happens to be a "Duchesse Somebody" or "Duke So-and-so," a "General," or even an "Empress," so be it—but don't ignore 'Just Joey'! And if it is the physical attributes that are most important to you, in the case of roses this is forgivable.

SOMETIMES ENGLISH ROSES PERFORM DIFFERENTLY IN AMERICA THAN THEIR CATALOGUE DESCRIPTIONS SUGGEST. 'LEANDER' SOMETIMES GROWS INTO A MASSIVE CLIMBER.

SPECIES ROSES

Roses have occurred naturally throughout the Northern Hemisphere for millennia. The earliest are known from fossils of the Oligocene epoch, thirty-five million years ago. Their range is from Alaska south to northern Mexico, across northern Europe, south to North Africa, and through Asia. Because of natural hybridization in the wild, the number of existing species is disputed; some are thought to be subspecies.

Most Species, or wild, roses are strong, vigorous growers, disease-free in climates suited to their requirements. Usually the flowers are single, often white or pale pink, and produced in great profusion in early summer. There are some yellow Species roses, mostly of Asian origin, and some double and even multi-petaled roses. There is a charm to their wildness, but they are usually best suited to large properties.

Rosa rugosa, the familiar "beach rose," is a species frequently used in gardens, and the lovely double yellow pom-poms of *Rosa banksiae* 'Lutea' have made the "Lady Bank's Rose" another popular choice. The "Cherokee Rose," *Rosa laevigata*, is widely grown in the South for its sweet, white, single flowers; it is the state flower of Georgia. *Rosa glauca* is one of the few roses grown more for its foliage than for its flowers: its blue-green leaves tinted plum and bronze are irresistible.

ROSA MOSCHATA PLENA CAN CLIMB HIGH INTO TREES, WHERE IT WILL CASCADE DOWN IN SWAGS OF INTENSELY PERFUMED, APPLE-BLOSSOM-WHITE FLOWERS. NO MATTER THAT IT BLOOMS ONLY ONCE A SEASON!

OLD GARDEN ROSES

Sometimes called simply "Old-Fashioned" roses, the roses extolled in literature since the very beginning of writing looked quite different from the florist roses we know today. The old roses generally bloomed only once in the season, with many flowers covering the entire bush for weeks. Their smaller blooms often held far more petals than do modern roses, and these petals were sometimes clustered tightly into gorgeous swirls. Their colors were usually soft pinks and magentas and deep mauves and vermilions. But more than anything it was their fragrances that immortalized them. When Juliet tells Romeo, "That which we call a rose by any other name would smell as sweet," she speaks of a fabulous perfume unknown among today's florist Valentine bouquets.

Many of the roses now called "antique" were popularly grown in France and England in the nineteenth century. During those remarkable hundred years French and British hybridizers produced a stunning array of new roses, grandparents and parents of the Modern roses most often sold today. (It is also worth noting that some catalogues list as "antique," "old-fashioned," or "heritage" many roses introduced as recently as the 1950s. As new generations of rose lovers come along, nostalgic references to "grandmother's garden" no longer stretch so very far back into the past.)

There are several categories of Old Garden roses. Those most frequently offered in catalogues are Gallica, Alba, Centifolia, Damask, Bourbon, and Moss, but specialty growers sometimes list additional subdivisions. China and Tea (or Tea-Scented) roses are exotics brought to Europe in the late eighteenth century to be hybridized with the European roses. You may see the heading "Cabbage Roses," which is not an official group but a reference to those ball-shaped blossoms packed with crinkled petals so popular in fabric designs and Victorian painted wallpapers. Then there are the groups of old Climbing roses—Noisette and Boursault in particular—but sometimes Climbing Tea and Climbing Bourbon as well.

When faced with such a bewildering array, just remember Juliet's admonition to Romeo: any and all of these roses under any name are wonderful.

Fortunately the past fifty years have seen a renewed interest in old roses, and today many catalogues offer hundreds of choices. Lists of these roses—named after kings, queens, presidents, heroic statesmen, and famously beautiful women—read like a romantic *Who's Who* of history.

To add these famous beauties to your shrub borders and flower beds is to bring a long-ago era of elegant garden parties and swashbuckling romance right into your own backyard.

GALLICA

Rosa gallica is one of the oldest European roses, known to the ancient Mediterranean world, but has come to be called the "French rose." Indeed the French hybridized thousands of cultivars beginning in the late eighteenth century.

Gallicas are usually sturdy, winter-hardy, suckering shrubs, once-blooming. Flower colors range from pale pink to deep maroon, but are mostly in lush rosy tones often blended and swirled. Because of the intense colors they are referred to as the "Mad" Gallicas. Their fragrance is legendary.

If grown on their own roots they will spread by suckers. A Gallica grafted onto a nursery rootstock will not sucker and is more useful in a small garden. Prune only for deadwood and slight shaping.

'Apothecary Rose' (*Rosa gallica officinalis*) An ancient Species rose; a tidy, suckering plant with large, fragrant, slightly double flowers shaded deep rose to ivory around golden stamens. Simple and deliciously scented. Before 1590.

'Belle de Crecy' A profusion of fragrant, velvety lilac-purple flowers. A short-statured suckering rose unless grafted, it is sometimes considered a Hybrid China. Before 1848.

'Camaieux' A striped rose that is pink and white, violet and pink, or rose and purple, often with all combinations on the bush at once. Flowers are loosely double and very fragrant. 1830.

'Cardinal de Richelieu' One of the darkest roses, with purple, mauve, crimson, and violet petals swirled tightly around a button center; fragrant. Low-growing on its own roots but as tall as 6' if grafted. 1840.

'Charles de Mills' Occasionally listed as 'Bizarre Triomphant,' this very old rose has flat, round flowers with many petals in shades of maroon, purple, and deep crimson on a loose, arching shrub to 4'.

'Duchesse de Montebello' Pale-pink flowers suggest Damask or Centifolia heritage, as does the arching growth habit of this deliciously fragrant rose.

'Empress Josephine' Named in the early nineteenth century to honor the woman who championed roses in her garden at Malmaison. The flowers are large, open, and sometimes frilled like peonies, and the colors are dark and light pink with violet shadings.

'Tuscany' Flowers are an extremely dark velvety red, almost black in some lights. This may be the "Velvet Rose" the herbalist Gerard wrote of in 1596.

'Ypsilante'/'Ipsilante' Its large flowers are pale pink, lilac, and blush-white, the petals bunched and gathered like fine China silk; fragrant. 1821.

THE "MAD" GALLICA ROSES ARE FAMOUS FOR THEIR VIVID BLENDS OF PURPLE, MAUVE, FUCHSIA, AND VERMILION. 'CHARLES DE MILLS' HAS THEM ALL, SWIRLED INTO A MASS OF PETALS PACKED FLAT AS FRAGILE SÈVRES SAUCERS.

ALBA

The origins of these roses are not entirely known. Albas may be the result of a natural cross between *Rosa canina* and the old *R. gallica* and/or *R. damascena* roses, and/or other Species roses.

Albas are generally graceful large shrubs, some reaching 8' in height, with similar spread. Their flowers are extraordinarily sweetly fragrant, white or pale pink. These roses are once-blooming. The foliage is an attractive matte grayish-green, a good addition to the range of greens in a garden. These roses are winter hardy to Zone 5, some to Zone 3, and are disease resistant. The only pruning necessary is of deadwood. An Alba should be allowed to attain its natural size and proportion.

'Félicité Parmentier' A tall, graceful plant whose soft-pink, multi-petaled flowers emit the classic Alba fragrance, reminiscent of fine scented powder. 1834.

'Great Maiden's Blush' (*R. alba incarnata*) This tall shrub reaches to 8', with an arching habit. Clusters of delicate pink, very fragrant flowers. Around 1738.

'Konigin von Danemark' Grows to about 6'. The deepest pink of the Albas, subtly shaded and glowing. The fragrance is remarkable. 1809 or 1826.

'Suaveolens' (*R. alba semi-plena*) One of the most fragrant of all roses, used since before 1750 in the production of rose oil in southeast Europe. Semi-double white flowers with bright-yellow stamens. Elegant bluish foliage.

CENTIFOLIA

The name refers to the many ("hundred") petals of this rose. Its origins are disputed. Sometimes it is listed as a naturally occurring wild rose in Europe and Asia, and sometimes reported to be the result of much hybridization during the seventeenth century in Holland. The characteristic flowers are often called cabbage roses, but that term is also loosely applied to any large, round, many-petaled rose.

Centifolias are medium-sized, winter-hardy, once-blooming shrubs with large, fragrant flowers usually in pink tones but ranging from white to deep rose, including striped and bicolored varieties. The weight

'GROS CHOUX D'HOLLANDE' MEANS "BIG DUTCH CABBAGE," A HUMBLE NAME FOR SUCH A LUSCIOUS PINK ROSE WITH A LEGENDARY FRAGRANCE.

of the flowers may bend the canes gracefully. The plants grow in a loose, arching habit to about 6'. Some smaller types reach only 4 or 5', with more upright growth. Allow Centifolias to attain their natural form, and prune only to remove deadwood or for occasional shaping.

'Blanchefleur' Introduced in 1835 by Jean-Pierre Vibert, who worked closely with Empress Josephine at Malmaison. The fragrant flowers are white with a tint of pale pink on a spreading shrub to 4' or 5'.

'Cristata'/'Crested Moss' Sometimes listed with the Moss roses. The flowers are especially fragrant, silvery-pink, and loosely gathered into a high center. Introduced by Vibert in 1827.

'De Meaux' A small rose with small flowers, but exquisitely charming. The foliage is petite, a perfect foil for the fragrant, pale-pink button flowers formed of many tiny petals. 1789.

'Gros Choux d'Hollande' Its French name, "Big Dutch Cabbage," refers to its cabbage-rose form. The flowers are very fragrant and very large and medium pink, containing many petals swirled into a ball. It makes an arching shrub to about 5'. Sometimes listed with the Bourbons.

Rosa centifolia/'Provence Rose' This is the rose correctly called the cabbage rose. Its medium pink flowers are extremely fragrant, cupped with many petals swirling and crumpled into loose balls. Before 1596.

DAMASK

These roses, whose name refers to the ancient city of Damascus, are thought to have hybridized naturally from *Rosa gallica* and *Rosa phoenicia* in Asia Minor and to have been brought to Europe by the Crusaders in the thirteenth century. Their fragrance is legendary. Damask roses have long been used to produce attar of rose, the most intensely scented rose oil and an indispensable ingredient in perfumes.

Damask roses are generally upright, gracefully arching shrubs from 5' to 7', their long canes weighted down with large, strongly fragrant flowers in colors from white to deep rose. They are generally once-blooming with a profusion of flowers during the season, well worth the space in the garden. A few, such as the 'Autumn Damask,' 'Quatre Saisons Blanc Mousseux,' and 'Rose de Puteau,' reliably repeat bloom. Some catalogues further divide this category into Damask Perpetuals and Portlands.

'Autumn Damask' Known by a variety of names, this very fragrant repeat-blooming rose of ancient origin may be the famous ancient Mediterranean "twice-blooming rose of Paestum." Deep-pink double flowers open from darker buds in profusion in summer and sporadically through the fall.

'Celsiana' This exquisite rose may have been popularly grown before 1750. Once-blooming and deliciously fragrant, the delicate satiny-pink flowers are wide open around beautiful golden-yellow stamens, displayed in abundance against grayish-green matte foliage.

'Comte de Chambord' Repeat-blooming with lovely silvery-pink flowers full of petals quartered and swirled around a deeper pink center, richly fragrant, on an upright shrub to about 5'. 1860.

'Hebe's Lip'/*Rosa damascena rubrotincta*/'Reine Blanche'/'Margined Lip' Highly praised for its fragrant white-cupped flowers, the edges of the petals just brushed with crimson. Very thorny and more compact than others. Believed to have been introduced around 1846, although some claim 1912.

TRANSLUCENT AS FINE FRENCH PORCELAIN, THE PETALS OF DAMASK ROSE 'CELSIANA' SURROUND BRILLIANT GOLDEN STAMENS. SOMETIMES DATED AS EARLY AS 1750, THIS ROSE HAS BEEN POPULAR FOR CENTURIES NOT JUST FOR ITS BEAUTY BUT FOR ITS DELICIOUS FRAGRANCE.

'Ispahan'/'Isphahan'/'Rose d'Isfahan'/'Pompon des Princes' Deep-pink buds in clusters open to silvery-pink cupped flowers. One of the most deliciously fragrant and longest blooming of the once-blooming roses, the bush is covered in bloom for many weeks in midsummer. Bluish-green foliage is attractive all season.

'Jacques Cartier' A compact plant with bright-green foliage and stunning pink carnation-form flowers. The late season and fall bloom is remarkable. Most often listed with the Portlands. 1868.

'Leda'/'Painted Damask' Sometimes white, tinged pink at the edges, sometimes a pale pink with less marked edging. Always lovely and very fragrant. Before 1827.

'Mme. Hardy'/'Félicité Hardy' Very fragrant. Nicknamed the "green-eyed bewitcher" for its pure white petals around a green button center. 1832.

'Quatre Saisons Blanc Mousseux'/*Rosa damascena bifera alba muscosa*
Sometimes listed as a Moss rose and called 'Perpetual White Moss,' this is a sport of the 'Autumn Damask.' Its flowers are white, in clusters, from mossy buds, very fragrant. It repeat blooms reliably, but not in great profusion.

'Rose de Rescht' Reintroduced in 1920 and believed to be a very old rose, this is one of the best garden roses, with a tidy habit, only about 3' tall, and very reliable repeat bloom throughout the summer. Pom-pom–shaped flowers are a rich, vibrant cerise-and-magenta blend, and fragrant.

'Trigintipetala'/*Rosa damascena trigintipetala*/'Kazanlik' One of the most fragrant of all roses, used since before 1689 in southeast Europe for attar of roses. Pale-pink wide open flowers have many petals loosely arranged around golden stamens on a wide, arching bush.

'York and Lancaster'/*Rosa damascena versicolor* This famous rose, grown before 1551, symbolizes the peace between the two factions in the War of the Roses. Bicolor pink and white, sometimes divided exactly down the middle. It is a large plant, in season covered with very fragrant flowers in profusion.

The origins of 'Ispahan' are debated. Sometimes listed as a Damask, and spelled variously 'Isfahan' and 'Isphahan,' it was grown in France at least as early as 1832 and may have come from Persia centuries earlier. Not in dispute are its many superlatives: most fragrant, longest blooming of the once-blooming roses, most beautiful of all pink roses. It has no peer as a focal point in the garden.

BOURBON

These roses developed on the Ile Bourbon, now Réunion, in the Indian Ocean. They are possibly a natural cross between China and Damask Perpetual roses. Their reblooming characteristic made them important in the French breeding programs after 1819, when the first seeds were sent to Europe. They were most popular up to the middle of the nineteenth century.

Bourbons often have arching growth and richly scented, gorgeous flowers with good repeat bloom, like the best of their China and Damask ancestors. Colors are white through pink to deep red. Prune only deadwood and for shaping.

Some of the Bourbons, for example 'Mme. Isaac Pereire,' give their best display when their long canes are gently bent outward in almost horizontal arching fashion and fastened to stakes. Called "pegging," this practice encourages flowering all along the canes. Bourbon climbers will be more floriferous if the canes are tied almost horizontally to a wall or trellis.

Some specialty catalogues offer a separate group of Hybrid Bourbons, which are not always repeat bloomers.

'Boule de Neige' Arching growth to about 6'. The pure white flowers open into snowball shapes. A good repeat bloomer and moderately fragrant. 1867.

'Coquette des Blanches' Fragrant white flowers on an arching shrub to about 6'. Very good repeat bloomer. 1871.

'Fantin Latour' Sometimes listed with the Centifolias, one of the most popular old roses for its profuse midseason bloom of deliciously fragrant, pale-pink double flowers. An arching shrub to about 5'.

'Irwin Lane' An extraordinarily fragrant rose whose flowers are large crimson globes in spectacular profusion when the canes are pegged or trained horizontally as a climber. Occasional repeat blooms.

'Kathleen Harrop' A sport of the beloved 'Zéphirine Drouhin,' this thornless climber has flowers of a more delicate pink, but the same fine climbing habit and an equally sweet scent. 1919.

'Mme. Ernst Calvat' Sometimes listed as a sport of the voluptuous 'Mme. Isaac Pereire,' with large lavender-pink flowers on long, arching canes. The best display is achieved by pegging the canes down. 1888.

'Mme. Isaac Pereire' One of the most extravagant roses. The extraordinarily fragrant, huge, voluptuous, many-petaled flowers are vividly but subtly shaded from deep rose-pink to magenta. If pegged down, the long, arching canes will produce a prodigious amount of blossoms. 1881.

Bourbon rose 'Reine Victoria' was hybridized in France but named for the Queen of England (in 1872). The epitome of the cabbage rose, its flowers are perfectly spherical and packed with petals and fragrance. Unfortunately, the foliage is prone to blackspot in humid areas.

'Reine Victoria' In mild climates this rose will bloom until very late fall, even into winter. It has deep-pink, ball-shaped flowers reminiscent of the cabbage roses popular on Victorian fabrics and wallpapers. This rose dislikes humid summers. 1872.

'Souvenir de la Malmaison' One of the most beautiful flowers imaginable, and rightly dedicated to Empress Josephine. Extremely fragrant satiny cream and pink petals in great profusion, tightly twisted into symmetrical patterns, adorn a small 2' or 3' shrub all summer. 1843.

'Variegata di Bologna' An unusual climber, with variegated cabbage-rose flowers striped crimson and purple against white. Fragrant, with occasional rebloom. 1909.

'Zéphirine Drouhin' This thornless climber is a good choice for around door-ways or along paths. In late May and June its deep magenta, loosely double, sweetly fragrant flowers are in great profusion. It repeat blooms throughout the season, the new foliage emerging a colorful bronzy red. 1868.

Moss

"Moss" refers to the texture of the fuzzy scent glands covering the buds and sepals of these distinct flowers. This sticky "moss" may be reddish, bronzy, chartreuse, or bright green, and is deliciously scented with spicy fragrances as varied as the blossoms. Touching it perfumes the fingers. Although the original Moss rose is thought to be a sport of a Centifolia, the traits of many other ancestors, particularly Damask, are evident. The deep colors of some cultivars suggest China roses in their lineage.

Because of extensive hybridization, bushes of Moss roses have many varying silhouettes, from short and stocky to tall and arching. Some bloom only once, some repeat, and all are fragrant. Prune only for deadwood or minor shaping.

'Alfred de Dalmas'/'Mousseline' This rose was hybridized in mid-nineteenth-century France and is sometimes listed as a Portland. The bush is tidy and lush, the flowers are large, loosely double, white-blushed pink, and are produced continually through late fall.

'Common Moss'/'Old Pink Moss'/'Communis' The pre-1600 original (as opposed to the many clones sold today) was almost always included in cottage gardens because of its great beauty. The flowers are pure pink and strongly perfumed, and the moss has a rosy-piney scent. It is once-flowering on a small, arching plant.

'Deuil de Paul Fontaine' One of the darkest roses, blackish-purple at its best, although strong sun will fade the colors to an interesting brown mauve. The buds are well mossed and the repeat bloom is reliable on this small, thorny, arching plant. 1873.

'Gloire des Mousseux' Huge clear-pink flowers fashioned from crumpled petals adorn this large plant, which reaches about 6'. Very fragrant and very well mossed; abundant flowers. 1852.

'Mme. Louis Leveque' Enormous clear-pink flowers rounded in the cabbage-rose fashion. In warm, dry sunshine it creates a stunning picture, but cool, rainy weather spoils the flowers. 1874 or 1898.

33

SOMETIMES CALLED THE MOST FRAGRANT ROSE OF ALL—RARE PRAISE INDEED AND PROBABLY DESERVED—'MME. ISAAC PEREIRE' HAS LUSCIOUS, VIVID PINK CABBAGE-ROSE BLOSSOMS ALL ALONG ITS ARCHING CANES AND THE FAMOUS PERFUME OF THE BOURBON ROSES.

'Nuits de Young' Dark violet, almost black, roses, perfumed both of flower and of moss, adorn a neatly growing shrub to about 5'. 1845.

'Oeillet Panachée'/'Striped Moss' A delicate, charming candy-striped rose. The flowers are small, composed of many ivory or blush-pink petals striped with crimson. Buds covered with bronzy moss. The bush is a petite 3'. 1888.

'Salet' Reliably repeat-blooming, and one of the most deliciously fragrant; not particularly mossy. The flowers, clear, bright pink, composed of many ruffled and frilled petals swirled together in the form of little peonies, are produced all summer in profusion. 1874.

THE FRAGRANCES OF MOSS ROSES ARE VARIED, FROM FRUITY TO SPICY TO PINEY, AND COME NOT ONLY FROM THE PETALS BUT ALSO FROM THE "MOSSY" SCENT GLANDS COVERING THE SEPALS AND BUDS. THIS EXAMPLE WAS SOLD UNDER THE NAME 'OLD RED MOSS,' BUT MAY HAVE BEEN KNOWN BY OTHER NAMES AT OTHER TIMES DURING ITS LONG HISTORY.

CHINA AND TEA

China roses are native to the warmer parts of Asia. All are repeat blooming and thus were indispensable to the nineteenth-century breeders who wanted to produce winter-hardy repeat-blooming roses. The 'Chinese Monthly Red' rose was sent to England from Calcutta in 1792. 'Parson's Pink China' arrived the following year. In 1810 'Hume's Blush Tea-Scented China' was imported, and in 1824 'Park's Yellow Tea-Scented China' arrived from a Canton nursery. Descended from wild Asian species, these four figured in the production of all Modern roses.

Tea roses are believed to be descended from China roses and *Rosa gigantea*, a large climbing yellow rose. The name Tea may have originally referred not to the fragrance but to the eighteenth-century European tea merchants doing business in Asia who were instrumental in exporting these roses to Europe. The characteristically high-centered flowers with their spiral arrangement of petals are familiar now in the Modern Hybrid Teas. Familiar, too, are the colors: white through ivory to yellow and orange, palest pink through rose to deep red, and blends capturing all the hues of sunrise and sunset. Added to the palette of the China roses, white through pink to dark red and even black-maroon, these imported roses offered fantastic hybridization possibilities.

Hybridizers in England, Sweden, and Italy all worked with China and Tea roses, but the most intense work was carried out in France. The colors and the repeat bloom of these exotic roses ensured their popularity, even if they were not hardy outdoors in most of Europe.

The original nineteenth-century Chinas and Teas have been lost and found throughout the generations since their introduction. Much creativity and guesswork go into matching the correct historic name to a plant found growing in an old garden.

China and Tea roses are twiggy plants continually producing new flowers all along their stems. China roses are compact and bushy, 2' to 4', while some Tea roses can become arching bushes to 7'. Both are best suited to mild climates, where they will bloom year round. Prune only for deadwood or slight shaping. Severe pruning will reduce the number of flowers.

'Archduc Charles' Grown since at least 1840, this rose has the Chinas' typically changeable colors in shades of pale to deep pink.

'Catherine Mermet' This famous old pink Tea was introduced in 1869 and is most often grown in greenhouses and sold as a florist flower. It will grow happily in a warm sunny spot in the garden. Flowers are exquisite in form, color, and fragrance.

'Cramoisi Superieur' This reliably repeat-blooming rose has stunning cupped crimson flowers with silvery lavender tints to the undersides of the petals. 1835.

'Devoniensis' Named for its place of origin, Devon, England, this extraordinarily beautiful rose is also known as the "Magnolia Rose" for its fragrance. Elegant pink-blushed buds open to large, creamy, quartered flowers tinted palest peach or yellow. A popular climbing form was introduced in 1858.

'Duchesse de Brabant'/'Comtesse de Labarthe'/'Comtesse Ouwaroff' One of the most widely grown of the old Teas, with cupped flowers of warm pink and an intense fragrance. In warm climates it makes a tall shrub to 6', with glossy foliage and an abundance of bloom. 1857.

'Mutabilis'/'Tipo Ideale'/*Rosa chinensis mutabilis* A large open shrub to 8' or more, constantly in bloom with graceful single flowers. Only slightly fragrant but remarkably colored. The flowers open pale yellow but turn to pink and then crimson, all the colors plus intermediary hues decorating the bush at once. At least as early as 1894.

'Old Blush' Introduced into Europe in the late eighteenth century and marketed as 'Parson's Pink China,' this historic rose played a significant role in the hybridization of modern roses. Constantly in bloom with loosely open pale-pink flowers that deepen in hue with age.

'Perle des Jardins' Fragrant, rounded blossoms packed with petals in sulfur, primrose, and yellow ivory on a compact plant with dark, plum-colored branches. A hardy grower in warm climates.

'Slater's Crimson China' Possibly the famous *Rosa chinensis semperflorens* introduced in England around 1790. Constantly in bloom with an abundance of cherry-red flowers.

Noisette

Despite the French name, these roses originated in Charleston, South Carolina, when in 1802 John Champney crossed a pink China rose with *Rosa moschata*, producing 'Champney's Pink Cluster.' He gave seeds from this plant to his friend Philippe Noisette, who successfully grew a rose with large clusters of double flowers. His brother Louis, a rose breeder in Paris, introduced this new 'Noisette' strain in France in 1815, and it became instantly popular. The yellow Tea roses, also new on the Paris scene, were crossed with Noisettes and contributed their color range and their longer canes, allowing Noisettes to be used sometimes as climbers. Some catalogues list the Tea-Noisette crosses separately.

Noisettes are excellent hedge roses and small to large climbers. They are usually repeat blooming, but because they keep growing late in the season their new growth is often too tender for severe winters. Prune only for deadwood and minor shaping, always allowing these long-caned roses to attain their natural graceful shape.

'Aimée Vibert' Extremely fragrant small white flowers in clusters on almost thornless stems. To about 5' tall and spreading at least as wide; the floral display repeats reliably. 1828.

'Blush Noisette' A good pillar rose or small climber, always in bloom with large sprays of loosely double lilac-pink flowers. 1817.

'Céline Forestier' This beloved rose makes a good small climber or large shrub to about 8', with light-green foliage and continual bloom of large, flat flowers filled with swirling petals in shades of pale yellow, cream, and ivory, sometimes shaded to peach. One of the French Tea-Noisette crosses. 1842.

'Champney's Pink Cluster' The original cross, from Charleston, South Carolina, in 1802. It will add to the garden not only history but deliciously scented, gorgeous, palest-pink flowers of semi-double to double form on a vigorous, bushy, tall plant.

'Crepuscule' Continually blooming and very fragrant, this 1904 Tea-Noisette produces romantic, loosely double, exquisitely tinted flowers, golden yellow and apricot fading to warmly tinged ivory. Best in mild climates.

'Gloire de Dijon' Sometimes listed with the Teas; more often considered a Tea-Noisette. The very fragrant flowers are large and flat, quartered with swirls of many petals tinted apricot and orange or buff pink, depending on the weather. Best in a mild, dry climate. 1853.

'Jaune Desprez'/'Desprez à Fleurs Jaunes' This Tea-Noisette produces flowers in clusters at the ends of long stems; colors vary from yellow to orange to apricot to creamy ivory, depending on the weather. The bush is vigorous, clothed in light-green foliage, with a long display of bloom. 1830.

'Maréchal Niel' A tender rose for very warm climates or the greenhouse, worth growing for its fragrant, large-cupped golden-yellow flowers that nod down from tall stems. Grown against a warm wall, it will flower all year. A Tea-Noisette cross. 1864.

'Mme. Alfred Carrière' One of the loveliest and most beloved climbers, carefree, vigorous once established, and not very thorny, with attractive bluish-green foliage and masses of white, loosely double, deliciously scented flowers, blushed pink in bud and at the center, all season. Remarkably cold-hardy for a Tea-Noisette. 1879.

'Nastarana' Extraordinarily fragrant, white-blushed pink flowers, continually in bloom all season, grace this large bush or small climber to 8' or taller. The scent is remarkable. 1879.

INTRODUCED IN 1879, THE NOISETTE 'MME. ALFRED CARRIÈRE' HAS NEVER BEEN SURPASSED AS A WHITE CLIMBING ROSE. EARLY FLOWERING AND RELIABLY REPEAT BLOOMING, ITS SWEETLY FRAGRANT BLOSSOMS EMERGE FROM PINKISH BUDS IN GREAT PROFUSION AGAINST THE ATTRACTIVE BLUE-GREEN FOLIAGE. IT CAN CLIMB HIGH INTO TREES, WHERE IT WILL FESTOON THE BRANCHES WITH SWAGS AND GARLANDS OF FLOWERS. WHAT'S MORE, THIS ROSE IS ALMOST THORNLESS, SO IT CAN BE GROWN NEAR DOORWAYS AND ALONG PATHS.

HYBRID PERPETUAL

These were the first successful repeat-blooming hybrids. In the mid-nineteenth century Hybrid Chinas and Hybrid Bourbons were crossed with Damask Perpetuals to produce hardy, vigorous, repeat-blooming roses with large, colorful flowers. Experiments continued, so the group shows great variety in growth habits: Some bushes are stiff and vertical, some are arching and spreading, and some have very long canes suitable for training along fences or for use as small climbers. Heights range from a few feet to 8' or more. Most of these vigorous roses form sturdy bushes densely covered with healthy foliage, and they are more winter-hardy than the Hybrid Teas. Hybrid Perpetuals, phenomenally popular during the Victorian era, usually have extremely showy flowers in a wide range of colors from tinted white through pinks, lilacs, and mauves to deep rose, fuchsia, dark red, and almost black maroon. Many are wonderfully fragrant.

Long-caned Hybrid Perpetuals are often pegged down, with the canes splayed out from the center of the plant and tied to stakes almost horizontally in a fountain effect. This method induces many more large blooms all along the arching canes. During the peak bloom season, no other rose display is as extravagantly lavish. However, their later cycles of bloom are never as impressive.

Today, gardeners who recognize the unique beauty of Hybrid Perpetuals grow them in mixed borders where the bloom sequences of other plants take over when the rose bushes are not in flower. These vigorous roses are happier in mixed borders than are the more finicky, longer-blooming Hybrid Teas. They add to the picture their special nostalgic blend of delicious fragrance and elegant flowers. Prune for deadwood and to shape. These bushes generally can be pruned severely and still bloom the same season.

'Arrilaga'/'Heinrich Munch' One of the famous big pink cabbage roses. Huge, beautifully formed, and perfumed glowing-pink flowers with large petals swirled around high centers adorn a large plant for the back of the border, to 6' or more. Can be used as a short climber. 1929.

OPPOSITE, ABOVE: 'BARON GIROD DE L'AIN' IS ONLY ONE OF THE STUNNING RESULTS OF THE NINETEENTH-CENTURY FRENCH QUEST FOR REPEAT-BLOOMING ROSES. THIS HYBRID PERPETUAL IS A FORERUNNER OF TODAY'S MODERN HYBRID TEAS. RICHLY PERFUMED, THE DARK RED BLOSSOMS HAVE IRREGULAR "TORN" EDGES TOUCHED WITH WHITE. OPPOSITE, BELOW: THE FLOWERS OF HYBRID PERPETUAL 'PAUL NEYRON' ARE AMONG THE LARGEST IN THE ROSE WORLD, SOMETIMES MISTAKEN IN BOUQUETS FOR PEONIES.

'Baron Girod de l'Ain' Instantly recognizable, the dark scarlet blooms are made up of many petals with seemingly torn edges tipped in white, the center cupped as if presented on a matching saucer. Unique fragrance, epitomizing roses. This is a good candidate for pegging, as the long canes can seem leggy if left growing upright. 1897.

'Baronne Prévost' The most reliably reblooming Hybrid Perpetual, and one of the most beautiful and lavishly perfumed. Large, silvery-pink flowers full of twisted petals in the old-fashioned quartered manner, with deeper and paler shadings, in continual display on a tall, sturdy, vigorous, thorny bush clothed in matte-green leaves. 1842.

'Général Jacqueminot' "General Jack" is the great-grandparent of many of today's red roses. Brilliant velvety crimson, perfectly formed flowers on a tall and leggy plant. Grow low perennials around its base and enjoy the show of gorgeous red flowers above. 1858.

'General Washington' This French rose honors the first American president. It is packed with fragrant petals in hues of deep rose, dark mauve-pink, and faded crimson, arranged in the typical lush Victorian manner. 1861.

'Hugh Dickson' The red flowers are huge, round, many-petaled affairs, the red of opera-house velvet, and with a luxuriant perfume. A good repeat bloomer. The long canes benefit from pegging. 1905.

'Marchioness of Lorne' This late-Victorian creation from England epitomizes the cabbage rose. Big, voluptuous, and seductively perfumed, with dark rosy-pink petals creating an open cup. A large plant that will produce extravagant flowers all along its canes. 1889.

'Paul Neyron' Incredibly huge, distinctively deep-pink cabbage-rose flowers, perfect for cutting on tall stems. Luxuriant scent. With generous feeding and watering, this plant will offer up the largest roses in the garden. 1869.

'Reine des Violettes' This mid-nineteenth-century rose is considered the bluest. Very much like a Gallica with its flat, petal-packed flowers in mauve, lilac, faded purple, and gray. The fragrance is unique, almost peppery.

MODERN ROSES

'La France,' introduced in 1867, is the first Hybrid Tea rose and marks the beginning of the era of Modern roses. In the mid-nineteenth century, hybridizers were mainly interested in producing roses that bloomed all summer long, either continually or in cycles, or at the very least that had a good repeat bloom in the fall.

Over time, other traits were wanted: disease resistance, superior hardiness, dwarf growth, ground-covering habit, ease of maintenance. Hybridizers tried to keep up with changing tastes, and the result was a confusing array of different categories of roses. Within the deceptively simply titled groups of Bush, Shrub, Ground Cover, and Climbing, there are the further divisions of Large-Flowered (or Hybrid Tea); Cluster-Flowered (Floribundas); and Polyanthas. There are in addition Hybrid Musk, Hybrid Rugosa, and English roses.

All these groups may be further divided, based on the nature of their blooms: a Climber might be a Climbing Tea or a Cluster-Flowered Climber, or for that matter a Climbing Miniature may be Large-Flowered.

It gets worse. Catalogues might also list Patio roses, Landscape roses, Tree roses, Pillar roses, Border roses, Bedding roses, Blanket roses, and Carpet roses. And so on.

Still, as overwhelming as this may seem, most rose catalogues are a pleasure to read or look through. Those with color photographs are the most accessible to the new gardener, but even those with no illustrations will become indispensable for their riveting descriptions.

Catalogues offer Modern roses under some or all of these categories: Hybrid Tea, Hybrid Musk, Polyantha, Floribunda, Rambler, Climber, Shrub, Rugosa, and Miniature.

If fragrance is important to you, look for that in the description. Don't assume a Modern rose will have a scent. With all the breeding for superior growing traits and fashionable colors, the famous old rose perfume got lost along the way. While there are certainly many fragrant Modern roses, their perfumes are not nearly as evocative as those of the old stars.

HYBRID TEA

All modern Hybrid Teas trace their parentage to 'La France' and the many early examples developed in the last quarter of the nineteenth century. They generally have large flowers, good repeat bloom, and a wide spectrum of color, including yellow and orange. For many years Hybrid Teas were the most popular of all roses, with hundreds of cultivars readily available in local nurseries and from mail-order catalogues. But in recent years the resurgence of popularity of the Old Garden roses and the interest in new English roses and the hardier and more disease-free Landscape roses have diminished their allure.

Occasionally certain Hybrid Tea roses will be listed under the category Grandiflora. This is a nonspecific category more often recognized in America than elsewhere, and may include Floribunda (Cluster-Flowered) roses as well. The criteria are large flowers borne singly or in clusters—a very general catch-all.

Some cultivars are prone to blackspot and mildew, depending on climate. Check catalogue descriptions for roses appropriate to your garden.

Hybrid Teas thrive on a program of attentive care and vigilance against disease and pests. Water frequently and deeply. A systemic insecticide may be used early in the season, following label directions, or dust regularly with rose powder and check frequently for diseased or damaged foliage. Feed with granular or liquid fertilizer, always following label directions.

Many Hybrid Tea roses benefit from severe pruning to keep them bushy and free flowering. The adage is to "prune waist-high in the fall, knee-high in the spring." This method gets the plant through the winter, and whatever die-back occurs can be groomed away in spring.

In areas of severely cold winters, you may need to mound soil and mulch into a small hill to cover the canes completely. Your local garden center will advise you on wintering roses in your area.

'Chrysler Imperial' One of the most fragrant, a classic dark-red rose perfect for bouquets. 1952.

'Dainty Bess' The most popular of the single Hybrid Teas. Satiny-pink petals arranged around deep-maroon stamens. The climbing version is equally stunning. 1925.

'Fragrant Cloud'/'Duftwolke' Famously fragrant, large coral-colored flowers from bright red buds. 1963.

'Just Joey' Huge, gorgeous, orange-and-apricot flowers; good fragrance. 1972.

'Miss All American Beauty'/'Maria Callas' This rose has dark, rich-pink flowers on long stems on a tall plant, and a very rich perfume. 1965.

'Mister Lincoln' A very popular dark-red rose, velvety crimson with almost black shadings; fragrant. 1965.

'Peace' One of the most famous roses, huge pale-yellow flowers with pink edges to the petals and tints of ivory and blush; very fragrant. 1945.

'Queen Elisabeth' Medium-pink flowers in clusters on extremely tall plants, a vigorous and healthy grower. 1954.

'Reichspraesident Von Hindenberg' Among the largest flowers, resembling peonies in size and shape. Pink and strongly perfumed. 1933.

'Tiffany' Beloved for half a century for its large classic blooms of yellow-tinted pale silvery-pink and its extraordinary Tea-Damask fragrance, as well as for its ease of cultivation. 1954.

THE FORMAL ROSE GARDEN EPITOMIZED: BOX-LINED PARTERRES PLANTED WITH 'QUEEN ELISABETH,' 'PEACE,' AND 'RED MASTERPIECE' AT THE DAVID AND ALICE VAN BUUREN MUSEUM NEAR BRUSSELS, BELGIUM.

Hybrid Musk

These roses, developed in the early twentieth century in England, are generally long-flowering plants that produce clusters of many small, sweetly scented flowers along long, arching canes. The bushes are excellent for informal hedges, for training along fences, and as short climbers. Remarkably vigorous and disease free, they reward very little care with an abundant display of flowers, repeat blooming well into fall. Of all roses, these are the most tolerant of shade, although like all roses they perform best in full sun. No special maintenance or knowledge of rose cultivation is necessary to grow these carefree, generous bloomers. Prune only for deadwood. Hybrid Musks should be allowed to attain their natural graceful shape.

'Ballerina' A favorite for its ease of cultivation and abundance of flowers. It is a small shrub, under 5' tall and as wide, with disease-resistant foliage and a phenomenal display of single pink, white-centered flowers in huge trusses. No fragrance. 1937.

'Bishop Darlington' Forms an arching bush to 6', with sprays of large, loosely double, well-opened flowers in shades of apricot, pink, and ivory-yellow; deliciously scented. Repeat blooms reliably all season. 1926.

'Buff Beauty' Abundant, multi-petaled, small ball-shaped flowers in tints of straw, yellow, and apricot, on long, arching canes with dark-green foliage; very fragrant. Slight shade improves the colors, as sunlight fades the blossoms quickly. 1939.

'Cornelia' A gracefully arching shrub to 6' with all-summer sprays of strawberry-pink and cream pom-pom flowers in profusion. Strongly scented. The foliage is bronze, sturdy, and glossy. 1925.

'Penelope' Very popular for its clusters of small, loosely double, ivory-yellow flowers sometimes tinted with peach, followed by striking salmon-pink hips after a fall bloom. 1924.

'Prosperity' Easily pruned as a hedge, with bright light-green neat foliage. Flowers are small ivory or blush pom-poms that blanket the branches. The main display lasts for weeks in June. Beloved since 1919.

POLYANTHA

These bushy, low-growing roses with clusters of small flowers first
became popular in the 1870s. Hybridizers crossed both Tea roses and
China roses with cluster-flowered Species roses to achieve repeat bloom.
The first Polyanthas were small plants ideal for small gardens, with
charming flowers in large clusters, one branch offering a pretty bouquet.
Over the years, fashion led to much bigger bushes with larger flowers;
these are now classed as Floribundas.

The smaller Polyanthas are good for flower beds, borders, and small
hedges. The taller varieties, which may reach 6' or more, are good as

The flowers of Hybrid Musk 'Lavender Lassie' are pink, not lavender, but they are
lush and fragrant, blooming happily in light shade, and the shrub is tall enough to
be a climber. Could you ask for more?

focal points or for tall hedges. Prune for deadwood or shaping. Most Polyanthas will bloom even if severely pruned.

'Baby Faurax' Richly colored violet flowers, strongly perfumed, on a small plant to 2'. 1924.

'Cécile Brunner'/'Sweetheart Rose' The flowers have the shape of tiny Tea roses, high-centered and deliciously scented, opening to a delicate pink, perfect in corsages or as boutonnieres. The bush can grow to 5' or more, and there is a popular climbing version. 1881.

'China Doll' A small bush with large, informal, bright-pink flowers tinted yellow. 1946.

'Clothilde Soupert' A wide, compact bush to 3' to 4', producing intensely fragrant old-fashioned–looking white flowers tinted cool pink. 1890.

'Happy' A tiny shrub, less than 2' feet tall, covered with sprays of small cherry-red flowers. Wonderfully cheery along a path, but with no fragrance. 1954.

'Marie Pavie' Intensely fragrant and very generous with double white flowers. A small plant, to about 3'. 1888.

'Perle d'Or' This plant can grow to 8' or more with age, but its flowers are as diminutive, charming, and fragrant as those of the 'Sweetheart Rose,' in pastel gold and peach with uniquely furled outer petals. 1884.

'Phyllis Bide' A small climbing rose with clusters of charming, informally double, freshly scented flowers in a blend of yellow, peach, and pink; never out of bloom. 1923.

'The Fairy' Extraordinarily hardy and vigorous, in bloom summer to frost with sprays of tiny, pink double flowers set off by dark, shiny foliage on arching canes. Perfect in borders, low hedges, mass plantings, as a single accent, even in containers. 1932.

'PHYLLIS BIDE' HAS REMAINED ONE OF THE MOST POPULAR ROSES OF ALL SINCE IT WAS INTRODUCED IN 1923. INCREDIBLY FLORIFEROUS EVEN FOR A POLYANTHA, IT REPEAT BLOOMS THROUGHOUT THE ENTIRE SEASON ON LONG CANES PERFECT FOR SMALL TRELLISES.

FLORIBUNDA

This group, sometimes called Cluster-Flowered roses, was developed from the Polyanthas as tastes led to larger flowers on larger bushes. The earlier hybrids, from the 1920s, were still small-statured plants, but now there are Floribundas to 6' or more, some with very large Hybrid Tea–like flowers. Their popularity comes from their hardiness and vigor, as well as from the remarkable range of colors available: crimson, orange, and pink to subtle blends of peach, apricot, violet, and tan. They are prolific bloomers, good as single specimens or for hedges. Prune for deadwood or shaping, or to keep a plant in bounds.

'Betty Prior' One of the most popular roses in America because of its ease of cultivation and generous all-season display. The flowers are bright pink fading to white at the center, in large clusters. 1935.

'Chuckles' This early Floribunda has the carefree vigor characteristic of the best of the group, producing masses of vivid pink, semi-double flowers; slightly fragrant. 1958.

'Europeana' Long popular because of its low, spreading growth habit and its all-summer profusion of scarlet flowers in large clusters. 1963.

ABOVE: DESIGNER LISA STAMM PLANTED THE POPULAR 'BETTY PRIOR' TO PROVIDE COLOR AND PRIVACY AROUND HER POOL. OPPOSITE: THIS WONDERFUL RAISED STONE BED IS AT FOLLY FARM, IN BERKSHIRE, ENGLAND. THE EVER-BLOOMING AND BELOVED WHITE ROSE 'ICEBERG' CROWNS THE WALL, WHILE OTHER PLANTS ARE TUCKED INTO POCKETS BETWEEN THE STONES.

'Eye Paint' A large shrub covered with geranium-scarlet single flowers, each with a white center around yellow stamens, produced in huge clusters. Long-lasting as cut flowers; one stem is a bouquet. 1975.

'Gruss An Aachen' One of the most fragrant, with old-fashioned, flat, many-petaled ivory-blushed pink flowers, tolerant of some shade. 1909.

'Iceberg' One of the best-selling roses ever, for this vigorous, disease-free large shrub covers itself with pristine white flowers all summer. There is an equally popular climbing version. 1958.

'Lavender Pinocchio' Unusual blendings of lilac, mauve, and tan grace the large flowers of this medium-sized shrub to 4'. Fragrant. 1948.

'Simplicity' Often hyped as a "blooming fence," this floriferous and easy-to-grow rose offers pleasant but not distinguished pink semi-double flowers in clusters all summer. 1978.

'Sunsprite'/'Friesia' Unusually fragrant for a yellow rose. The color is a clear, deep, true yellow; the bush is large, to about 5'. 1977.

Rambler

These are long-caned, vigorous roses that can be trained to sprawl along a fence or climb up posts or into trees. Most are once-blooming. They were originally bred from large-growing wild species such as *Rosa wichuriana*, *Rosa sempervirens*, *Rosa arvensis*, and *Rosa multiflora*. The most intense hybridization took place in the early 1900s, and the new cultivars with larger flowers and sometimes with repeat bloom eventually came to be called Large-Flowered Climbers. As with the Climbing rose category, the Ramblers include roses of many different lineages with many different flower types but all sharing the characteristic long canes and sprawling growth habit; the two categories overlap. A rose you are seeking may be listed as a Rambler in one catalogue and as a Climber in another.

Choose the vigorous roses from this group to cover pergolas and arbors, to screen unsightly walls or fences, to create informal hedgerows, or to provide romantic backgrounds for wild gardens.

'Albertine' A very popular climber, with extremely fragrant, loosely double pastel-pink flowers in abundance over a long period in summer. 1921.

'Baltimore Belle' Exceptionally fragrant and elegant very double pale-pink flowers in clusters, with good repeat bloom. 1843.

'Belle Portugaise' Needs a mild climate but where it is hardy it puts on a spectacular display, climbing high into trees and cascading down in clusters of pale-peach old-fashioned–looking flowers. 1903.

'Blush Boursault' Stunning, delicate pink-and-blush flowers with many petals gathered together informally into large balls. Mid-1800s.

'Carnea' One of the most fragrant, double pale-pink flowers on a vigorous plant. 1804.

'Félicité et Perpetué' Deservedly popular for over 150 years for its clusters of delicately perfumed, very double small white flowers in elegant sprays on a vigorous plant with dark green foliage. 1827.

CALLED THE "BLUE RAMBLER," 'VEILCHENBLAU' IS BLUE ONLY IN CERTAIN LIGHTS, AND THEN ONLY FOR A MINUTE. ITS MASSES OF SMALL PURPLE AND MAUVE FLOWERS QUICKLY FADE. BUT THE EFFECT OF THE PROFUSION OF SO MANY SHADES OF VIOLET IS STUNNING, ESPECIALLY CONTRASTED WITH THE VIVID SUNSET COLORS OF 'WESTERLAND' OR THE SNOWY WHITE OF 'ICEBERG.'

'Gardenia' Rampant new growth covered with fresh-scented ivory flowers reminiscent of gardenia blossoms. 1899.

'May Queen' A reliable, vigorous, long-caned plant with very double medium-pink flowers in profusion. 1899.

'Veilchenblau'/"Blue Rambler" Profuse clusters of small violet, mauve, and white flowers that fade in the sun to lilac-gray. Grown in slight shade, which it will tolerate, and with just the right lighting, the flowers can look blue. 1909.

CLIMBER

This group became popular only in the second half of the nineteenth century. *Rosa wichuriana*, a Species rose sometimes called 'Memorial Rose,' was bred with hybrids to introduce larger size and stronger colors in climbing roses, and along with the Multiflora began a race of climbers in England and America.

Climbing roses as a group include many diverse forms united by the characteristic of having very long canes. There are Climbing Hybrid Teas, Climbing Floribundas, even Climbing Miniatures. Ramblers are often listed as Climbers.

Roses are not actually capable of attaching themselves to a support. They do not twine, nor do they have tendrils or suckers. Some huge-growing Species types are able to climb unaided into trees by sheer massive, rapid growth, and their thorns do, to a certain degree, hold them in place. But most roses need the help of gardeners to stay affixed to a trellis, fence, arbor, or porch roof. Pliant new canes can be woven in and out of latticework. Once the wood hardens it will stay in place. Canes can also be fastened with twine, wire, or masonry staples.

Many modern Climbers are reblooming, but check the catalogue description to avoid disappointment. Once-blooming Climbers flower on old wood or the previous year's growth, and should not be pruned except immediately following the bloom season. In general, prune only dead-wood or for minor shaping.

OPPOSITE, ABOVE: VIVID, VIGOROUS, DISEASE-FREE 'WESTERLAND' IS A CLIMBING FLORIBUNDA THAT CAN BE AN IMPRESSIVE FREESTANDING SHRUB WITH LARGE INFORMAL BLOSSOMS LUMIN-OUSLY TINTED WITH HUES OF APRICOT, PINK, AND YELLOW. OPPOSITE, BELOW: ONE OF THE FINEST RED ROSES, 'DUBLIN BAY' OFFERS UP CLUSTERS OF FLOWERS THAT ARE A VIVID SEALING-WAX RED, INHERITED NO DOUBT FROM 'ALTISSIMO,' ONE OF ITS PARENTS, A GREAT RED CLIMBER ITSELF.

'Altissimo' Brilliantly vivid red single flowers on stiff, upright branches, resembling a red clematis. 1966.

'Awakening' A sport of the famous 'New Dawn' with all its best characteristics and the added beauty of fully double quartered blossoms. 1935.

'Blaze' Long the most popular climber in America, with vivid red flowers and an iron constitution. Reintroduced in 1950 in a more reliably repeat-blooming version sometimes called 'Blaze Improved.' 1932.

'Clair Matin' A vigorous grower with bronzy-green foliage and clear-pink loosely double flowers with dark-golden stamens. 1960.

'Dublin Bay' This fine climber is a seedling of 'Altissimo' with double red flowers that last well in the vase. 1969.

'Golden Showers' One of the best yellow climbers, with continual sprays of informal pastel-yellow flowers accented by maroon stamens against shiny bright-green foliage. 1956.

'New Dawn' Beloved for its charmingly disheveled, pale-pink, sweetly scented flowers produced in great profusion against shiny, disease-free foliage. Can become enormous, capable of covering a small cottage. 1930.

'Parade' A sport of 'New Dawn,' and equally sturdy, with large, dark-pink flowers on long stems, suitable for cutting. Blooms profusely, even under adverse conditions, and will even bloom in shade. 1953.

'Viking Queen' A popular pink climber, a vigorous, hardy plant with deep rosy-pink, old-fashioned flowers and good fragrance. 1963.

'Westerland' Sometimes listed as a Climbing Floribunda, this extremely hardy and disease-free rose can be a large, freestanding shrub. It has sturdy, tall, woody canes, glossy foliage, and vivid orange flowers highlighted with gold, peach, and salmon. 1969.

Shrub and English Roses

The category of Shrub roses was created by the American Rose Society to include a wide variety of roses that are not necessarily related but share winter hardiness and disease resistance and are reliable repeat bloomers.

The very popular English Roses are grouped in this category, but some catalogues list them separately or with the newer French Renaissance™ and Danish Generosa™ roses. David Austin began breeding his English Roses in the 1970s, with the goal of recapturing the charm and fragrance of the old roses but on shrubs that would be hardy, vigorous, and repeat blooming. Imitation is the highest form of flattery, but these roses have a distinct appeal and should be considered as something quite apart from the old roses and in no way a substitute for them.

'Belle Story' Huge, peony-shaped flowers delicately tinted pink and peach. 1984. English.

'Bonica' Sometimes listed as a "landscape rose," this super-hardy, disease-free shrub covers itself all summer with masses of charming, peachy-pink semi-double flowers. 1981. Shrub.

'Brown Velvet' Vivid crimson, orange, and brown blend on a vigorous shrub with shiny, dark-green foliage. 1975. Shrub.

'Constance Spry' Very popular for its large pink cabbage roses, despite its once-blooming habit. 1961. English.

'Golden Wings' A vigorous, dark, glossy shrub covered continuously with very fragrant, single, pale-yellow flowers arranged around prominent amber stamens. 1956. Shrub.

'Hawkeye Belle' Very hardy, vigorous plant with large, fragrant "old-fashioned" flowers tinted pale pink and salmon. 1975. Shrub.

'Heritage' Vigorous tall bush with profuse pale-pink globular blooms. 1984. English.

'Leander' Profuse, very double apricot flowers on a tall, vigorous plant. 1982. English.

'Mary Rose' Large, clear-pink, very double flat flowers all summer. 1983. English.

'Raubritter' Always popular for its small, perfectly round, pink cabbage-rose flowers in sprays. 1936. Shrub.

'Sea Foam' Sometimes listed with the Ramblers, 'Sea Foam' flaunts a continuous display of masses of small, white, double flowers in huge sprays on arching canes, perfect for cascading over a low wall. 1964. Shrub.

'William Shakespeare' Very dark red petals fill flat, very double, fragrant flowers. 1987. English.

RUGOSA AND HYBRID RUGOSA

The beloved fragrant "wild" beach roses, *Rosa rugosa*, growing on sandy dunes along the Atlantic and Pacific coasts of North America are actually of Japanese origin. They have large, open, single flowers of deep pink or white, and produce fat, round, colorful hips in fall. Rugged, winter-hardy without protection, disease resistant, tolerant of drought and even of shade, and not favorites of deer, Rugosas make excellent hedges and thrive in mixed-shrub borders. They even manage happily and showily as highway plantings.

Because of these admirable traits, they have been used in hybridizing hardy, carefree shrubs called Hybrid Rugosas. Generally these roses share the same rugged constitution as the Species Rugosas but often have showier flowers.

All Rugosa roses and their hybrids tolerate, but do not require, severe pruning. The Species varieties tend to be stoloniferous, which means they spread by runners and can colonize large areas. For this reason they are a popular choice on sand dunes to help control erosion, as their root system can become massive. Sometimes Hybrid Rugosas spread by runners as well.

In general, the Rugosas do not like foliar sprays (pesticides or fertilizers sprayed on the leaves). The leaves will burn and turn brown, and the bush will take a while to recover. Luckily, Rugosas rarely show any signs of diseases that would require spraying.

OPPOSITE, ABOVE: MODERN SHRUB ROSE 'CAREFREE' LIVES UP TO ITS NAME. PLANT IT, WATER IT, AND NEVER WORRY ABOUT DISEASE OR DEADHEADING. OPPOSITE, BELOW: 'HERITAGE' HAS BEEN ONE OF DAVID AUSTIN'S MOST POPULAR ENGLISH ROSES SINCE ITS 1984 INTRODUCTION. IT FORMS A VIGOROUS, UPRIGHT BUSH TO 7', COVERED ALL SUMMER WITH LARGE, CUPPED, SHELL-PINK FRAGRANT FLOWERS.

Rosa rugosa alba White-flowered, typically rugged, with large, single, deliciously fragrant flowers and edible hips.

Rosa rugosa rubra Pink-flowered, in hues from medium to vivid deep pink. Large, single flowers produce edible hips.

'Belle Poitevine' Gorgeous pink to mauve, large, loosely double fragrant flowers on a shrub to 6'. 1894.

'Blanc Double de Coubert' One of the most deliciously scented roses, double white and abundant. No hips. 1892.

'Conrad Ferdinand Meyer' Stunning, enormous, cool-pink Hybrid Tea–shaped fragrant flowers on a very tall, very thorny plant that can be used as a short climber. 1899.

'F. J. Grootendorst' Small, garnet-red carnation-shaped flowers in clusters, not fragrant. 1918.

'Flamingo' Huge, flaring, single, bright-pink fragrant flowers on a tall shrub to 8'. 1956.

'Frau Dagmar Hartopp'/'Fru Dagmar Hastrup' A smaller shrub to 3' or 4' with exquisite silky, cool-pink, sweetly scented single flowers, dark-red hips, and healthy, lush foliage. 1914.

'Moje Hammarberg' A rugged bush with beautiful foliage and fragrant, large, semi-double, purple-pink flowers with golden stamens. 1931.

'Rose à Parfum de l'Hay' One of the most fragrant roses, with large opera-velvet–red flowers of Hybrid Perpetual form on a tall, thorny bush. No hips. 1901.

'Roseraie de l'Hay' A stunning large shrub with lush growth and intensely fragrant, magenta-pink double flowers in profusion. No hips. 1900.

'Thérèse Bugnet' Dark-red canes add winter interest, and there is a long summer display of bluish-pink, richly scented double flowers followed by colorful fall foliage. 1950.

DON'T OVERLOOK THE FALL DISPLAY OF ROSE HIPS WHEN MAKING YOUR SELECTION. HIPS COME IN MANY COLORS, SHAPES, AND SIZES AND CAN EXTEND THE SEASON OF INTEREST WELL INTO WINTER. *ROSA RUGOSA* IS PARTICULARLY VALUED FOR ITS HIPS.

62

A MOST UNUSUAL HYBRID RUGOSA, 'CONRAD FERDINAND MEYER' IS A STIFF, UPRIGHT CLIMBER
WITH IMMENSE FLOWERS THAT COULD PASS FOR THOSE OF A HYBRID TEA.

ABOVE: A SURPRISINGLY LITTLE-KNOWN HYBRID RUGOSA, 'MOJE HAMMARBERG' IS COMPACT
AND PROUDLY DISPLAYS TYPICAL RUGOSA FLOWERS—LARGE, VIVID MAGENTA, AND INTOXICAT-
INGLY FRAGRANT. BELOW: HYBRID RUGOSAS ARE AMONG THE EASIEST ROSES TO GROW,
UNTROUBLED BY BLACKSPOT AND NOT FAVORITES OF DEER. 'ROSERAIE DE L'HAY' IS ONE OF THE
MOST BEAUTIFUL, ITS HUGE MAGENTA-PINK FLOWERS APPEARING VIOLET IN CERTAIN LIGHTS
AND EMITTING AN INTENSE AND INTOXICATING FRAGRANCE.

MINIATURE

Miniature roses may have the bloom characteristics of any of the roses in their parentage, and are classified in this group based on their size alone. The flowers are in proportion to the plants, usually less than 1½" across.

The first Miniature roses were discovered in China and introduced in Europe around 1818. A great many cultivars were available in the early nineteenth century up until about 1840, but then they began to fall out of commerce. The Miniatures sold today are bred from 'Oakington Ruby,' 'Tom Thumb,' and the Species *Rosa rouletti*, which was found growing in a window box in the town of Mauborget in Switzerland in 1919.

Miniatures may be grown outdoors in containers and hanging baskets as well as in the ground. Grown indoors in containers, they will provide color and fragrance for a short time, but generally do not fare well as long-term houseplants.

Miniature roses are usually grown on their own roots, so outdoors they should be planted slightly deeper than in the container in which they were purchased. In containers their small, shallow root system tends to dry out quickly and requires frequent watering.

Severe pruning will keep them bushy and attractive and ensure an abundance of bloom. In late winter or early spring, cut all the stems back to the lowest outward-facing growth buds. If a larger plant is desired, cut all stems back by one half. Most Miniatures have very twiggy growth habits with many small branches, so pruning is a time-consuming task.

Miniature roses have their devotees. Popular cultivars include the tiny, almost thornless 'Cinderella' with its blush-white, fragrant double flowers; 'Dresden Doll,' often considered the prettiest because of its fragrant, round, double old-fashioned silky-pink flowers; the histori-cally significant 'Oakington Ruby,' a parent of many modern miniatures, loved for its tiny deep-red double flowers; and 'Tom Thumb,' long popular for its abundant display of Lilliputian red flowers on a plant small enough for a tiny pot.

OPPOSITE, ABOVE: PETITE BUT VIVID, 'HAPPY' (NAMED FOR ONE OF SNOW WHITE'S COMPAN-IONS) IS SOMETIMES CONSIDERED A DWARF POLYANTHA, SOMETIMES A MINIATURE. LESS THAN 2' TALL, IT CLOTHES ITSELF HEAD TO TOE WITH CHERRY-RED POM-POM FLOWERS; PERFECT FOR BORDERING A PATH. OPPOSITE, BELOW: ONE OF THE MOST BELOVED MINIATURE ROSES, 'MAGIC CAROUSEL' BLOOMS PROFUSELY, ITS WHITE PETALS EDGED IN SHADES OF BRIGHT CERISE THROUGH PINK TO BLUSH. ITS FLOWERS ARE ABOUT 1½" ACROSS.

3 Growing Roses

TO CHOOSE THE perfect spot in your garden for your roses, spend some time noticing which areas get the most sunlight. Roses thrive in rich, well-drained soil in a sunny location with regular watering. No matter where you garden within the temperate zones, the quality of the soil and the amount of sunlight combined with diligent watering will, more than any other factors, affect your success with roses.

GETTING STARTED

Roses may be ordered from mail-order catalogues or purchased at local nurseries and garden centers. There are advantages and disadvantages to either choice.

Mail-order catalogues offer a fantastic selection. If you are seeking an unusual rose that has caught your fancy, most likely you will need to order it by mail. The large, nationally marketed nurseries regularly update their offerings in all categories. Specialty nurseries offer rare roses and ones that have fallen from popularity; a few will even grow a hard-to-find rose on request.

Some mail-order roses are shipped in containers, but by far the most are shipped dormant and bare-root, either in early spring or late fall. This means that you receive a rose with leafless canes that have been cut back to about 5" and with loose roots wrapped in damp newspaper or raffia, protected by a plastic bag. The rose will be tagged with its name, but other than that there is no indication that the leafless skeleton will ever be anything resembling the beautiful flowering rose you ordered. This takes a little getting used to, but once you have had some experience with bare-root roses you will find that your imagination and expectation will carry you through to June.

If you order bare-root roses, have the holes prepared in advance, so that the roses can be planted right away. Then all that is required is patience and watering.

'LEONARDO DA VINCI' IS TYPICAL OF THE FLORIBUNDA ROSES, WITH ITS SPRAYS OF LARGE, SUMPTUOUSLY COLORED BLOSSOMS.

Local nurseries and garden centers will not have the extensive selection available by mail, but will enable you to see the roses' growing habits, which may affect your selection. Some local nurseries and garden centers sell bare-root roses, often in cardboard tubes wrapped with plastic, but usually you will get a plant growing happily in a container.

Look for sturdy, healthy green canes, fresh, spotless foliage, and firm buds. A few yellow leaves should not deter you, as roses grown in containers are subject to the caprices of spring weather. They will perk up and grow dramatically once planted.

A containerized rose can be planted any time during the growing season, but it is best to do so early enough to permit it to establish itself before winter comes.

Most roses available either by mail or at nurseries have been grafted, spliced onto the hardy roots of some other rose. There is usually a prominent knobby shape evident where the roses have been attached. This

A DRAMATIC ALLÉE OF ROSES IS ACHIEVED WITH A SERIES OF ARBORS AT ELIZABETH PARK IN HARTFORD, CONNECTICUT.

practice is popular with growers because it makes it possible to achieve a saleable-size rose quickly. The drawbacks are that the root system of the other rose may sometimes send up shoots that take over, and sometimes the graft union is weakened in severe weather.

Some growers do offer "own-root" roses. These may be smaller than grafted roses, but generally own-root roses are hardier and longer lived, and there is no chance of reversion to a different rootstock. Be sure you know if your rose is grafted or own-root, because this will affect the planting method.

Either way, never let the roots dry out. Bare-root roses should be unwrapped as soon as they are received and put in a bucket of room-temperature water. The branches, too, should be kept moist. Plant the roses within a day. Roses in containers should be kept well watered until they are planted.

SELECTING AND PREPARING A SITE

The ideal site would get full sun all day long, be open enough to allow gentle breezes for good air circulation but be protected from strong winds, and have rich, fertile soil that is frequently watered and well drained. If you are lucky enough to have such a spot in your garden, you may begin immediately to enjoy your roses, but most gardeners will have to approximate the ideal growing conditions.

The soil must be easily dug, loose, and friable. If it is hard packed and stony, you must amend it. Work in plenty of compost, well-rotted manure, peat moss, or garden sand. Also test the soil's pH, which indicates its acidity or alkalinity. Roses prefer slightly acidic soil with a pH of about 6.0–6.5.

PLANTING YOUR ROSES

Ideally, have the soil prepared and the holes ready in advance. For each rose dig a hole about 2' deep and 2' wide. The soil you dig out should be kept near the edge of the hole, ready to be gently returned over the rose's roots. Have a garden hose ready alongside the hole. You will want to be able to provide a gentle stream of water after the rose is planted.

Most roses are extremely thorny. Wear long sleeves and thick gloves. Some gloves designed especially for working with roses have long plastic shields that extend up the forearm, protecting your arm from scratches and your shirt from being torn.

If you are planting bare-root roses, first carefully replace some of the soil you have dug out to form a raised cone in the center of the hole. Don't press or firm it down. Amend it if necessary to refine the texture. Hold the rose in the hole to judge the depth at which it should be planted. If it is grafted, the knobby union should be just above the ground level in mild areas and just below the ground level in cold regions. Own-root roses should have all the root system below the ground level and just the stem and branches above. Cut off any damaged or broken roots, drape the root system over the cone of soil, and fill in loosely with the remaining soil, until the roots are completely covered and the soil is about an inch below the level of the surrounding ground. Do not press down.

THE HEALTHY FOLIAGE OF ROSES CAN BE EXTRAORDINARILY BEAUTIFUL. CAREFUL TENDING AND VIGILANCE WILL KEEP BLACKSPOT AND MILDEW AT BAY. SOME ROSES, SUCH AS *ROSA GLAUCA*, ARE GROWN MORE FOR THEIR FOLIAGE THAN FOR THEIR FLOWERS, AND A FEW OTHERS OFFER REMARKABLE AUTUMN COLOR.

Place the nozzle of the hose at the edge of the hole and with a gentle flow—more than a trickle but less than a stream—flood the hole. Let it drain, and flood it again. Repeat once again. This is sometimes called "muddying in," and its purpose is to make sure there are no air pockets around the roots, without compressing the loose soil you so carefully prepared. When the water has drained, fill in the shallow hole with the remaining soil up to the level of the surrounding ground. Do not press down. Mulch very deeply, at least 4".

If you are planting a rose that is in a container get it out of the container with as little root disturbance as possible. Hold the container in one hand, secure the soil around the roots with the other, turn it over, and shake firmly until the plant comes out. Once the plant is out of the container stand it upright. If the root ball holds its shape, place it in the hole so that the surface of the soil on the plant is at the same level or a little below the level of the surrounding ground, and fill in gently with the prepared soil. Sometimes when you remove a rose from a container the soil will fall away from the root ball, leaving bare roots. If this happens, plant as for a bare-root rose. Water as above, muddying in three times to eliminate any air pockets. Mulch well.

Water a newly planted rose frequently to ensure it does not dry out.

FERTILIZING

Roses love to be fed. A program of regular fertilization, accompanied by generous watering, will produce strong, healthy bushes. Many commercial fertilizers are available. You can choose between granular, which should be spread around the plant and worked into the soil before being watered in, and liquid, which can be mixed in a container and poured around the base of the plant or mixed in a hose attachment and sprayed on the foliage as well. Follow directions on the label. Never spray any strong fertilizer on the foliage of Rugosa roses. The leaves will burn.

Wait to begin fertilizing a newly planted rose until the foliage is growing freely. For established roses, fertilize as soon as new leaves appear in spring, and continue through late summer. This may be August, September, or even later, depending on what zone your garden is in. Let your roses to go into dormancy gradually before a severe frost hits.

Species and the vigorous Rugosa roses do not need fertilizing.

CARE AND MAINTENANCE

Roses thrive on generous watering, but the soil must be well drained. Continually wet soil, especially in winter, can be lethal for most roses.

Ideally, use a soaker hose, which will water the root system without getting the foliage wet. Using a sprinkler system is fine as long as the watering is done early enough in the day so that the leaves can dry before evening. Rose foliage that is constantly damp, especially on cooler nights after hot, damp days, is more prone to mildew and blackspot, the two main rose diseases. Rain, of course, will wet the foliage, but except in continually damp and humid conditions normal rainfall is not a problem. Just do not add to it with sprinkling in the evenings.

Except during prolonged droughts and very hot stretches, and in hot, dry climates, a deep watering twice a week is sufficient. Roses grown in containers need to be watered every day.

Some roses, particularly Species roses and Rugosa types, require very little maintenance. Occasional pruning of deadwood and general shaping, if desired, are all that is necessary. Rugosa roses may be severely pruned without ill effects if a smaller bush is desired, but do this in late fall or early spring before the plant leafs out. Old Garden roses, too, and many Ramblers, Hybrid Musks, and Climbers can thrive with little pruning. Deadheading (cutting off old blossoms that have faded) improves the look of roses but is not necessary. Where rose hips are desired, as for example on the Rugosa roses, leave the flowers on the bush to go to seed.

Other roses, in particular the Hybrid Teas, require considerable tending and grooming. Severe pruning, deadheading, and systemic or foliar controls against blackspot, mildew, and insects may be necessary, depending on the vigor of the rose and your particular climate. These special needs are noted in the descriptions in Chapter Two.

PESTS AND DISEASES

Just as roses have always inspired the deepest passions in gardeners, so have the pests that attack roses. Jean-Pierre Vibert, the celebrated nineteenth-century rose breeder who worked closely with Empress Josephine, said at the end of his long life in 1866 that there were only two things he hated profoundly: the English, for overthrowing Napoleon, and the white worms that destroyed his roses.

There are many animals and insects that enjoy your roses as much, if not more, than you do. The particular culprits will vary from one area to another. Ask about them at a local nursery or garden center.

The largest animals that may cause you problems are deer. Deer adore roses. They are especially fond of nibbling flower buds the day before you expect them to open into beautiful flowers, and they do not at all mind thorns. If deer are common in your area the only totally reliable protection is a 14' deer fence or two shorter fences placed about 4' apart around your entire property. If this is not practical, there are repellent sprays, but they may do as much damage to some roses as do the deer themselves. Individual rose bushes may be protected by netting or fencing, but this destroys the attractiveness of the plant. Rugosa roses seem to be the least appealing to deer.

Another way to repel deer is to encircle the rose or rose bed with plants deer do not like. Generally plants with pungent or aromatic foliage, such as lavender, nepeta, santolina, artemisia, caryopteris, perovskia, and common garden sage will work to a certain extent. Often

THIS MAGICAL ROSE GARDEN AT FOLLY FARM IN BERKSHIRE, ENGLAND, IS ONE OF THE FEW SURVIVING CREATIONS OF FAMED LANDSCAPE DESIGNER GERTRUDE JEKYLL.

plants with silvery or furry foliage are repellent to deer. Also, deer find all plants of the allium family, including garlic and chives, distasteful.

Rabbits can also be a problem, eating thorny branches and new buds. Hot pepper sprays deter rabbits. You may also chop up very hot chile peppers, onions, or garlic and sprinkle the bits around the base of the roses. Be sure to wear rubber gloves when handling chiles, as the potent juice will burn your hands, especially if they are scratched from rose thorns.

The most common insect problems are aphids and Japanese beetles, both of which can be combated with insecticides, but you can also fight them in less toxic ways. Aphids can be washed off with a powerful spray from the hose. Usually natural garden predators such as ladybugs will keep the aphid population down.

Japanese beetles are more difficult to deal with. They spend the winter as grubs under the surface of the soil, then emerge as flying beetles in midsummer to eat and mate until fall. The beetles can not only turn all the rose leaves to lacy skeletons, but will also devour each new bud of a repeat-blooming rose until early fall. Milky spore powder, which is lethal to the Japanese beetle grubs but harmless to anything else in the garden, can be applied to lawns and gardens as a deterrent. The problem is that it takes several years to start to work and unless everyone in the area is using it, the emerging beetles will fly over to your roses from neighboring properties. There are also traps that attract flying beetles with simulated flower fragrance and pheromones, but some people feel these only bring more beetles into the garden.

New insecticides made from the neem tree of India are coming on the market. The fruits and foliage of this tree are lethal to Japanese beetles, but harmless to humans and animals. In fact, the neem tree is an important food product in India, both for humans and livestock. Look for it as an ingredient in environment-friendly pesticides.

Another solution is to grow roses that bloom only once. They put on their lavish display in June, before the beetles start feeding. Old-fashioned once-blooming roses are generally hardier and more tolerant of severe weather than the modern hybrids, have graceful growing habits and attractive foliage, and for several weeks boast a floral display and fragrance few modern roses can match.

Occasionally rose catalogues caution that a particular rose "may be susceptible to powdery mildew" or "prone to blackspot." Avoid these roses if you live where summers are hot and humid. The foliage of all roses can suffer in humid weather, so those roses known to be susceptible will fare especially poorly. A chalky white coating on rose leaves indicates powdery mildew. Blackspot manifests as brown or black blemishes on the leaves, eventually turning them entirely yellow and then brown. Rose bushes easily survive minor attacks of either mildew or blackspot, but the infestation is unsightly and will spread if not checked. There are sprays, powders, and systemic preventives. Most of these contain chemicals of questionable environmental consequences. Enquire at your local garden center as to which products are recommended for your area. Follow label directions carefully.

You can prevent serious mildew or blackspot by carefully tending the roses and using nontoxic homemade remedies. The most important step is to remove any damaged or diseased leaves as soon as you see them, including leaves that have fallen to the ground. Do not add these to the compost. Discard them with your garbage.

A regular schedule of spraying the foliage with a half-and-half mixture of skim milk and water is said to prevent blackspot. A bit of liquid dishwashing soap will help the spray adhere to the leaf surfaces. Try alternating this mixture with a spray of water and baking soda for added effectiveness. Any preventive spraying should be done early on a dry day, so that the foliage may dry before evening.

Many roses have extremely healthy and disease-resistant constitutions and will not require any special treatment. The Rugosa roses and most Rugosa Hybrids in particular are rarely troubled by foliage diseases.

4 Roses in the Landscape

THE WORDS "rose garden" conjure up a nostalgic vision of many varieties of roses growing in orderly, impeccably weeded, well-mulched beds, with no other plants competing for attention, water, or nutrients. Paths might weave through these colorful plantings, bringing visitors close enough to inhale the most fragrant roses but keeping them at a safe distance from the largest, thorniest climbers. Small rose bushes line the foreground while behind them larger shrubs arch and sprawl, all against a backdrop of trellises or posts festooned with cascading climbers. For a few miraculous weeks in early summer, such rose gardens have no equal.

This is certainly a viable choice for a rose fancier, especially if the roses to be grown are the fussier Hybrid Teas or Hybrid Perpetuals, but for most small gardens today the space that would be taken up for just a few weeks of spectacular bloom cannot be spared. There are thousands of roses to choose from that will bloom all summer, but for all roses the main display is from late May to early July, depending on where you garden. From earliest spring until May, and from late summer until frost, a garden of only roses will be bare of much color.

Most roses do prefer to have a part of the garden solely unto themselves. They will achieve their optimum size and shape if no other plants encroach upon their territory. But additional color may safely be added by small spring bulbs, such as scilla, muscari, and chiondoxa, which will bloom and be gone before the roses leaf out. Small-statured alliums, and even common chives, bring later spring color and are actually beneficial companion plants, as they deter rabbits.

Low-growing groundcovers such as nepeta extend the flowering season, blooming along with the roses. The blue or lilac of many nepeta flowers are complementary to any color rose, from white through pink to deep red, even to yellow, orange, and salmon hues. The pungent foliage of the nepetas also deters some animal pests. The entire rose bed could be edged in lavender, which will bring all-summer interest and

'BLAZE' WAS THE MOST POPULAR RED CLIMBING ROSE IN AMERICA FROM 1932 UNTIL 1950, WHEN A CLONE WAS FOUND WITH EVEN BETTER REPEAT-BLOOMING QUALITIES. THIS IS 'BLAZE IMPROVED,' AND IT WOULD BE HARD TO IMAGINE ANY FURTHER IMPROVEMENTS.

additional fragrance. Lavender's silvery foliage and pale-violet flowers complement roses of all colors and, like nepeta, deter deer and rabbits.

Trailing or spreading annuals can also be used as an underplanting in a rose bed to add color. Honey-scented white sweet alyssum would enhance any color rose. Nasturtiums would jazz up hot red, yellow, and orange roses. Vivid blue lobelia helps paint a romantic picture under pink, mauve, or red roses and is absolutely stunning under white, yellow, or orange roses.

More and more gardeners are thinking of roses as plants to include in a mixed border. Most Old Garden roses, Shrub roses, Ramblers, and Hybrid Musks lend themselves to mixed borders, as long as they do not become overgrown by neighboring plants. The taller varieties should be planted at the back of the border or in the center of a bed. Smaller bushes and the many modern hybrid "landscape roses" can be sited with the same considerations needed for any other perennial of equal size. Miniatures can be used to line paths or to outline large beds.

Keep in mind the sunlight needs and watering requirements of roses when including them in mixed beds. Avoid shady areas, and don't plant roses in dry patches where drought-tolerant plants thrive—these may be injured by the generous watering roses require.

Roses make exceptionally beautiful hedges. In some parts of the world large, thorny Species roses are used to keep cattle, sheep, or horses from roaming. It was in the hedgerows of the island of Réunion that the 'Autumn Damask' rose grew alongside the China rose and is believed to have naturally hybridized with it to produce the Bourbon roses. 'Sweetbriar' makes a beautiful hedge in colder climates, while the exquisite "Cherokee Rose" provides a thorny, vigorous barrier in milder climates. For smaller properties, the Ramblers and Hybrid Musks are good choices for hedges. Rugosas make thorny and informal hedges. A long row of the lilac-blue 'Veilchenblau' would be a memorable sight. A small garden could have a proportionately small hedge of Miniature roses.

A rose may also be chosen as a specimen shrub in a lawn. The aggressively vigorous Climbing 'New Dawn,' left to its own devices and with nothing on which to climb, will mound up upon itself into a tall, cascading fountain of thorny branches covered for a long stretch of summer with freshly scented, charmingly disheveled pale-pink flowers in great profusion. A more spectacular focal point is hard to imagine. Less rampant but equally stunning would be a single bush of 'Ispahan.' This ancient Persian rose is hardy and disease-free, with dense bluish foliage, as beautiful out of bloom as in. For most of June and into July it covers itself top to bottom with very double, satin-pink, intensely fragrant flowers.

The reliably constantly blooming pink 'Heritage' makes a lovely, tall, upright statement as a specimen plant. Orange-and-peach 'Westerland,' which can be a climber, forms a sturdy and wide specimen 8' wide and as tall, covered all summer with cycle after cycle of sunset-colored flowers.

Climbing roses grace arbors, pergolas, colonnades, and bare walls. Tall varieties can also be grown up into trees, from which they will cascade down in colorful swags and sprays. 'Mme. Alfred Carrière' is a gorgeous climber, nearly thornless, with attractive matte bluish foliage and deliciously fragrant, very double cream-colored flowers all summer, sometimes pink-blushed in cool weather. It loves to climb trees, from which its long canes will erupt, laden with flowers high up against the sky. 'Zéphirine Drouhin' is a famous old climber, beloved for its thornless canes that allow it to be planted alongside paths where its vivid old-rose–colored flowers can be admired for their rich perfume. 'Paul's Himalayan Musk' reaches high into trees. When it blooms, for a long time in midsummer, it seems a cloud of pink caught in the branches.

On the windswept island of Nantucket, off the coast of Massachusetts, there is a small village called Siasconset. Here lovely old shingled cottages are entirely hidden beneath vigorous climbing roses that have surrounded them, grown up their walls, and met in a tangle on top of their roofs. Branches are pruned away from doors and sometimes but not always away from windows. When these ancient, massive rose bushes are in bloom around the old leaded-glass windowpanes, with a bit of lace curtain and the painted globes of old gas lamps just visible through the delicate pink-and-white blossoms, all the nostalgia and romance of the rose is called vividly to mind.

ABOVE: AT THE WORLD-FAMOUS OLD WESTBURY GARDENS, WESTBURY, NEW YORK, A MUTED
PALETTE IS ACHIEVED BY COMBINING BLUE-AND-WHITE DELPHINIUMS AND WHITE PEONIES
WITH OLD-FASHIONED PINK ROSES. BELOW: IN HER MATTITUCK, NEW YORK, GARDEN, ELLEN
COSNER GROWS THE ROMANTICALLY INFORMAL CLIMBING 'NEW DAWN' OVER A RUSTIC FENCE
AND GATE AS A BACKDROP FOR HER BEDS OF OLD-FASHIONED PERENNIALS.

ABOVE: LADY'S MANTLE, SEDUM, AND BLUE SPRUCE BLEND BEAUTIFULLY WITH THE DEEP-PINK
FLOWERS OF THIS GRACEFULLY CASCADING ROSE IN COSNER'S GARDEN. BELOW: POSITION A
GARDEN BENCH IN THE MIDST OF YOUR ROSE DISPLAY, SO THAT VISITORS CAN PAUSE TO
LUXURIATE IN THE FRAGRANCES AND COLORS, AND PERHAPS BE CARRIED AWAY BY NOSTALGIA
FOR OTHER ROSE GARDENS PAST.

EFFECTIVE COLOR COMBINATIONS

The gorgeous colors of roses, from pristine white through all the shades of pink to deep rose, dark velvety red, and purple, and from palest pastel yellow through deep yellow, peach, and amber to vivid orange, and the array of possible blendings of all those hues, allow for memorable juxtapositions with many other perennials and annuals in the garden.

The classic rose garden includes no other plants. The rose bushes are arranged in neat rows or some geometric pattern, carefully spaced to allow each bush its own space, and the soil is heavily and attractively mulched. But today's gardeners mix roses into perennial beds or shrub borders, incorporate them into nostalgic cottage gardens, and use them as bedding plants, groundcovers, and hedges. In this manner, roses become just one element of the garden picture.

Choosing appropriate colors for companion plants may seem the most important factor, and it really depends on your personal taste. All that matters is whether the companion plant wants the same garden conditions as roses and whether it will grow happily alongside without encroaching on the rose's space. Most importantly, will it bloom in your garden at the same time as the rose?

Groundcovers and very short plants are the best choices for growing close to the rose. Their roots will keep the soil around the rose loose and receptive to water. Two feet or more away from the rose's spread, slightly taller perennials may be used. Large perennials or small shrubs should be planted at enough of a distance so that their stems or branches will not sprawl over the rose. Tall shrubs and trees must be positioned far enough away so that they do not shade the rose.

Blue, lilac, lavender, and purple flowers complement all the colors of roses. The many shades of nepeta flowers are all wonderful backdrops when that plant is used as a groundcover. Bright royal-purple verbena 'Homestead Purple' spreads so rapidly it will form a stunning carpet under roses in one summer. Where happy, from Zone 6 south, it is a perennial. Annual blue lobelia can be a vivid edging plant. Perovskia, caryopteris, and blue or purple buddleias are good choices for background shrubs.

White flowers as well may be paired with any color rose. Alyssum 'Snow Crystals' makes a pretty and sweetly scented groundcover in any rose bed. White daisies, baby's breath, achillea 'The Pearl,' and white

ageratum are other choices for small or medium-sized companions. Buddleia 'White Profusion' is a good background plant.

Pink and red flowers look wonderful with white and yellow roses but may compete unfavorably with pink and red roses unless their hues are compatible. Pale saponaria blends well with red roses. Geum and annual red verbena do not, but paired with yellow roses they make a vivid "hot" bed.

Pale-yellow flowers usually look great with almost all roses, but bright yellows need a strong dark-red, purple, or vivid-orange rose for balance. The bright-yellow buttons of tansy add an old-fashioned note to a garden bed planted with red roses.

Some foliage plants are stunning with roses, especially those with silvery leaves. Many artemesia varieties are good foils for dark-red and purple roses, making them appear even more vivid. Silvery lamb's ears (*Stachys lanata*), lavender, and the tropical plectranthus are lovely with old-fashioned pink roses.

MANY ROSES ARE WELL SUITED FOR PERENNIAL AND SHRUB BORDERS, BUT THEY DON'T LIKE OTHER PLANTS CROWDING THEM. SPACE THEM WELL FOR MAXIMUM SUNLIGHT, AIR CIRCULATION, AND ELBOW ROOM.

'NEW DAWN' IS ONE OF THE MOST POPULAR PINK CLIMBERS, DESERVEDLY SO FOR ITS PROFUSE DISPLAY OF CHARMINGLY DISHEVELED, SWEETLY FRAGRANT, SHELL-PINK FLOWERS. DESIGNER LISA STAMM USES IT HERE ON PYRAMID TRELLISES, WHERE IT BLENDS HARMONIOUSLY WITH HER CAREFULLY SELECTED PERENNIALS.

COMPANION PLANTINGS FOR ROSES

Companion plantings are perennials, annuals, shrubs, or trees that harmonize with and complement one another when grown together.

PLANT	COLOR
Abelia grandiflora	White. Shrub
Ageratum	White, mauve, blue. Annual
Alyssum	White, mauve, purple. Annual
Buddleia	White, pink, violet, blue. Shrub
Caryopteris	Blue. Shrub
Cerastium	White. Perennial
Ceratostigma plumbaginoides	Blue. Perennial
Cornflower	Blue. Annual
Hardy geranium	White, pink, violet, blue. Perennial
Laurentia	Blue. Perennial
Lavender	Mauve. Perennial
Lobelia	Blue. Annual
Nasturtium	Yellow, orange, red. Annual
Nepeta	Blue. Perennial
Perovskia	Blue. Shrub
Petunia	White, pink, violet. Annual
Sanvitalia	Yellow, orange. Annual
Saponaria officinalis	Pink. Perennial
Spirea	White, pink, fuchsia. Shrub
Verbena	Mauve, violet, pink, red. Annual
Violets	White to blue. Perennial
Weigela	White, pink. Shrub

ABOVE: HUGH JOHNSON'S INSPIRED PERENNIAL GARDEN AT SAILING HALL IN ESSEX, ENGLAND,
INCLUDES OLD-FASHIONED PINK ROSES. BELOW: CASUALLY LUSH, 'CLIMBING NEW DAWN' HAS A
FRESH, SWEET SCENT ENTIRELY SUITED TO ITS CHARMINGLY DISHEVELED SHELL-PINK
FLOWERS. OVERLEAF: FLOWERS AND HEDGEROWS LINE ENGLAND'S CHARMING COUNTRY ROADS.

5 Roses Indoors

ROSES ARE garden plants. They need full sun, good air circulation, regular watering with excellent drainage, and a change of season to keep them happy. After a long summer of blossoming, roses gradually settle into dormancy as the temperatures drop, and then during the winter months they enjoy their well-earned rest. They are not easily grown indoors in heated, dry conditions.

In milder climates some roses, such as the Chinas and Teas, may go on blooming all year without a dormant period. These roses can be grown indoors, but they prefer a greenhouse environment.

Some of the Miniature roses can successfully be grown as windowsill plants for a short time. If dug in the fall after they have gone dormant, they can be induced to bloom in the house in winter and provide color and fragrance. But they will not be happy for long. Normal household conditions, even in a sunny south-facing bay window, do not meet their climatic needs. They will not have adequate sunlight or air circulation; it will be too hot for them; their shallow roots will quickly dry out, or rot in a saucer of water or wet sand and pebbles. Most indoor containers are too small; a Miniature rose needs at the very least a one-gallon container, and larger is preferable. The soil indoors will not have the organisms and bacteria that keep outdoor soil loose and rich, and indoor pests such as spider mite will become troublesome. With room fans, grow lights, a watering system that allows the soil to drain completely but never dry out, and chemical pesticides, however, the rose may survive.

CUTTING ROSES

Roses are best enjoyed indoors as cut flowers. As such, they have no rivals. They have been cherished as indoor decorations for millennia, and now that they are grown the world over for the cut-flower trade there is never a week throughout the year that they are not available. Most of the greenhouse-grown roses for the cut-flower market lack the

ANY COMBINATION OF ROSES MAKES A STUNNING BOUQUET, FROM THE MOST FORMAL FLORIST RED ROSES IN A SILVER VASE TO THE MOST CHARMING OLD-FASHIONED ROSES IN A HAND-PAINTED SUGAR BOWL.

strong fragrances of garden roses, cut that morning and brought right into the home, but they are available in endless colors and color combinations and sizes and shapes.

The classic bouquet of long-stemmed red roses has never lost its cachet, but it is only one of an infinite variety of floral arrangements to be fashioned from roses, with or without other flowers and foliage.

For fragrance, the Old Garden Gallicas, Bourbons, Centifolias, Albas, and Damasks can't be equaled, but they do not have the long, straight stems of florist roses. They make charming, romantic, nostalgic bouquets, either by themselves or mixed with other old-fashioned flowers such as buddleia, verbena, salvia, and Queen Anne's lace.

Cut these roses in the early evening or early morning, when they are most fragrant and before the heat of the day has faded them. Cut them at all stages of opening, from full buds to almost spent blossoms, for a naturally charming arrangement. For a formal arrangement, choose only full buds and slightly opened flowers.

Use sharp, clean clippers, scissors, or a knife. Ideally, cut the stem at a 45-degree angle just above a leaf node. Try to make a clean cut; a ragged tear may invite disease. Have a bucket of warm water with you, and as you cut your roses quickly place the cut stems into the water. Keep the cut roses out of direct sunlight.

Before arranging, remove the foliage, and if possible the thorns, that will be underwater in the vase. Make a new cut a little higher up the stem at an extreme angle so that a large cut surface may accept water. Try not to damage the surface of the stem.

The size of the container will govern the length of the stems needed, or conversely the roses you pick might determine which sort of vase is appropriate. Try the intensely perfumed silvery-pink 'Ispahan' in a silver teapot, perhaps with a few stalks of vivid blue *Salvia guaranitica* tucked in. Velvety black-red 'Tuscany' looks stunning with white 'Boule de Neige.' 'Mme. Alfred Carrière,' double creamy white sometimes tinged with pink, paired with buddleia 'Ellen's Blue' makes a delightfully fresh and fragrant small bouquet, perhaps in a painted fine porcelain vase.

The fragrances of some roses will be strong enough to perfume a room. Bouquets can be enhanced with sprigs of lemon verbena, pineapple sage, eucalyptus, or scented geranium foliage.

Broadleaf evergreen foliage makes a dramatic foil for the velvety flowers of roses. A branch of *Magnolia grandiflora* will provide a mirror-shiny, dark-green background for any color rose.

Roses can also be incorporated as minor notes in mixed bouquets. Dark-red 'Hugh Dickson' is a stunning accent in a vase of pastel-pink peonies such as 'Pillow Talk.' Sunset-orange 'Westerland' brightens up an arrangement of buddleia 'Ellen's Blue,' perhaps with the addition of a few stalks of tansy.

All roses are superb in bud vases. One full bud of 'Cécile Brunner' in a tiny vase with a sprig of jasmine and a ferny leaf of bronze fennel is a fragrant bedside-table welcome in a guest room.

ROSES RETAIN MUCH OF THEIR FRAGRANCE IF DRIED CAREFULLY, MAKING THEM EXCELLENT ADDITIONS TO POTPOURRI. PETALS AND COMPLETE BUDS MAY BE USED. EXPERIMENT TO SEE WHICH OF YOUR ROSES OFFER THE MOST PLEASING SCENTS WHEN DRIED.

SOURCES

VISIT THESE websites and order catalogues from the following nurseries. The websites and catalogues include many glorious color photographs, as well as growing information, which will help you make your selections.

THE ANTIQUE ROSE EMPORIUM
9300 Lueckmeyer Rd.
Brenham, TX 77833
(800) 441-0002
www.antiqueroseemporium.com

ARENA ROSES
P.O. Box 3570
Paso Robles, CA 93447
(888) 466-7434
www.arenaroses.com

ASHDOWN ROSES
P.O. Box 308
Landrum, SC 29356
(864) 468-4900
www.ashdownroses.com

HEIRLOOM ROSES
24062 NE Riverside Dr.
St. Paul, OR 97137
800-820-0465
www.heirloomroses.com

JACKSON & PERKINS
1 Rose La.
Medford, OR 97501
(877) 322-2300
www.jacksonandperkins.com

VINTAGE GARDENS
2833 Old Gravenstein Hwy. S.
Sebastopol, CA 95472
(707) 829-2035
www.vintagegardens.com

WAYSIDE GARDENS
1 Garden La.
Hodges, SC 29695-0001
(800) 845-1124
www.waysidegardens.com

WINDSWEPT GARDENS
Robert Bangs
1709 Broadway
Bangor, ME 04401
(207) 941-9898
www.windsweptgardens.com

OPPOSITE, ABOVE: 'TAUSENDSCHÖN' MEANS "THOUSAND BEAUTIES," AN APT NAME FOR THIS RAMBLER THAT COVERS ITSELF HEAD TO TOE WITH THOUSANDS OF BRIGHT-PINK BLOSSOMS THAT QUICKLY FADE TO WHITE. OPPOSITE, BELOW: ONE OF A TRIO OF FABULOUS ROSES INTRODUCED IN 1980, 'HONOR' (THE OTHERS ARE 'LOVE' AND 'CHERISH') HAS FLOWERS WITH THE GORGEOUS HIGH-CENTERED SILHOUETTE CHARACTERISTIC OF HYBRID TEAS. THEY ARE GARDENIA-WHITE WITH A TOUCH OF PALE YELLOW IN THE DEEPEST FOLDS OF THE PETALS.

INDEX